'As a clinical psychologist, I meet a lot of shame in the consulting room. Shame about body image, internet use or addictions. People who have been shamed for leaving a cult. And deep shame about who we are.

This book reveals biblical insights, including how Jesus dealt with shame. Cozens also describes how communities of Christians can help to get rid of shame and minister to the shamed.

I feel no shame in highly recommending this very helpful book.'
Dr Debbie Hawker, clinical psychologist

'Shame is everywhere, a powerfully emotional and painfully confusing experience that has the power to eat away at communities, our personal character and our confidence.

In this powerfully liberating book, Simon Cozens not only helps us to understand shame, but points us to the One who heals and restores.

Well written and timely, this book is Simon speaking from experience into a culture and context in which shame is too often hidden or misunderstood. I commend it to all, including those involved in prayer ministry, helping to bring freedom to others.'
Mitch (Keith Mitchell), evangelist and co-founder of Crown Jesus Ministries

'Shame is universally debilitating and has crippled humanity since the fall. Simon Cozens' brilliant and timely book is theologically rich, culturally relevant, missionally focused and pastorally liberating. Here is hope and help for a crisis of our times.'
Simon Ponsonby, Pastor of Theology, St Aldates Church, Oxford

'Simon Cozens addresses a feature of human experience that is universal but is so often hidden away. He demonstrates that the experience of shame was no less real for the great Augustine of Hippo as it was for the author himself as a sixteen-year-old witnessing the break-up of his parents' marriage. And herein lies the great value of this book: first, it reassures the reader that each individual's inevitable experience of shame places him or her in community. Second, the answer lies in the model of Jesus, who lived to take away guilt and shame "because he blew up shame itself" (p. 143). Every Christian should read this eminently readable book and should then share its wisdom with non-Christian friends.'

Professor Peter G. Riddell, Melbourne School of Theology, and School of Oriental and African Studies, University of London

'This is honestly one of the most thought-stirring and very possibly game-changing books that I have read recently, and I'm a prolific reader. Shame is a significant part of our lives, and Simon's book is a much-needed catalyst to bring it more openly "to the table" for discussion, not only in the church or in how we present the gospel but also in our own lives. You'll want to read this book several times, first to dive into the well-developed, biblically rooted truths that Simon presents, but then again, and probably again, to allow the Spirit to use these truths for his transforming work in your own life.'

Susan Sutton, International Director, WEC International, and author of *A Quiet Center*, *A Sure Path*, *Vision of the Deep* and *Designer Living*

'This book is a landmark and original contribution for understanding how shame affects all of us. Drawing richly on his own experience, Simon Cozens weaves stories, biblical insights and thoughtful questions, to force Western readers, time and again, to have another look at the misconception that shame only affect Asian societies. Highly recommended for leaders and cross-cultural workers open to new correlations between our personal and communities' shame and the claims of Jesus and the gospel.'

Kang-San Tan, Director, Baptist Missionary Society World Mission

Simon Cozens has worked as a computer programmer in the UK, been part of a team planting new churches in Japan and taught prospective missionaries at a Bible college in Australia. While in Australia, he began to explore the role of shame in Asian cultures, in Western society and in his own life. Since writing this book, he has returned to the UK with his wife, Henrietta, and their two children, Caitlin and Luke. He now leads a think tank within his mission agency, WEC International, helping them to explore what mission could look like in the future.

LOOKING SHAME IN THE EYE

LOOKING SHAME IN THE EYE

A path to understanding,
grace and freedom

Simon Cozens

INTER-VARSITY PRESS
36 Causton Street, London SW1P 4ST, England
Email: ivp@ivpbooks.com
Website: www.ivpbooks.com

First published 2019

British Library Cataloguing-in-Publication Data
A catalogue record for this book is available from the British Library.

ISBN: 978–1–78359–920–2
eBook ISBN: 978–1–78359–921–9

Set in Minion Pro
Typeset in Great Britain by CRB Associates, Potterhanworth, Lincolnshire
Printed in Great Britain by Ashford Colour Press Ltd, Gosport, Hampshire

*Inter-Varsity Press publishes Christian books that are true to the Bible and that
communicate the gospel, develop discipleship and strengthen the church for its
mission in the world.*

*IVP originated within the Inter-Varsity Fellowship, now the Universities and Colleges
Christian Fellowship, a student movement connecting Christian Unions in universities
and colleges throughout Great Britain, and a member movement of the International
Fellowship of Evangelical Students. Website: www.uccf.org.uk. That historic association
is maintained, and all senior IVP staff and committee members subscribe to the
UCCF Basis of Faith.*

Contents

Acknowledgments

I'm so immensely grateful to all the people who have walked with me on this journey of shame and recovery.

My wife Henrietta and our children have been models of loving acceptance, and have made me the man I am today.

My colleagues, students and friends at Worldview Center for Intercultural Studies in Tasmania have been an amazing source of support and encouragement.

While I don't want to embarrass him, one person deserves a special mention: almost all the decent ideas in this book are either due to, or have come out of conversations with, Christoph Ochs. Chris, it's been an amazing collaboration; thank you.

Thanks also to Peter Riddell at Melbourne School of Theology for encouraging us in our investigations of shame and encouraging me in my writing, and to all the team at InterVarsity Press for helping to steer that writing in the right direction.

My church, Family Church in Launceston, has taught me what it means to be real before God and before the world. The men's breakfast group have been my brothers and comrades in this fight. Thank you, Rob, David, Nick, Darren, Patrick, Col and many others. 'When friends by shame are undefiled, how can I keep from singing?'[1]

Introduction: shame uncovered

I was sixteen years old when I got the letter.

My father had left home a few months before and moved in with someone else. I had seen him a couple of times over the summer, but since then he'd gone strangely quiet.

1994 was a big year for me. I'd become a Christian a couple of years earlier through the witness of some friends at school, but 1994 was the year my faith really came alive – much to my parents' bemusement. While they were getting divorced, I was getting baptized. I was playing in a Christian rock band, and I even dragged my dad along to our first evangelistic concert. A few weeks after that, we had had some tough conversations about what the Bible says about divorce and adultery.

Come to think of it, that was the last time I saw him.

And then came the letter. I wasn't expecting to receive a letter from him, and I certainly wasn't expecting to read what the letter said. The neatly typed words told me that I was a disappointment to him. That I was an embarrassment to him. That I should leave him alone and never try to contact him again. I was standing in the kitchen of my mother's house when I read it. The shock hit me like a punch in the gut. I adored my dad as I was growing up; he was my hero. I thought he loved me.

I spent the rest of the summer trying to work out what I'd done wrong. How had I let him down? Was I not smart enough, not strong enough, not confident enough for him? Had I been too aggressive in my faith? I know now that, even if I had been, that doesn't justify what he did. But when you're a child, you just assume that adults are in the right. If they mistreat you, it must be because you deserved it. You never think they might be the one with the problem.

Disappointing. Embarrassing. Unlovable.

You're possibly expecting me to say that I started to think about myself like that, that I felt like I was a disappointment, an embarrassment, that I didn't deserve to be loved; that, from then on, my shame profoundly affected my identity. Well, no . . . and yes. The truth is that I never really *felt* those things at all. Jesus taught us to forgive those who sin against us, so I prayed that I would forgive him. And I honestly thought that *because* I'd forgiven him, I was going to be all right. I don't remember feeling abandonment or rejection. I certainly don't remember feeling ashamed.

In fact, I became really good at not *feeling* anything.

I've heard that soldiers in battle can be so driven by adrenaline that they don't notice their wounds until the fight is over. I think I must have battled against my feelings for the next twenty years. That's probably why I never stopped to realize quite how much insecurity, self-doubt and shame came to define me. Looking back, it all makes sense; I can see how my behaviour over those years was driven by my unconscious needs for acceptance, for attention and for love.

At the time, all I knew was that I needed people to take notice of me. I needed to do well in school; to be the smartest, the most interesting person in the room; to stand out from the crowd. I showed off and I cut other people down to try to make myself seem more impressive – not a great strategy if you want people to like you! I worked hard in my professional life and built my own 'personal brand'. But it never satisfied me. I always wanted more. Just like the Australian football coach Ian Watson:

I could bury my real shame behind the success and popularity that made me feel good. The more success I had, it made me more driven to be more popular. I was in a repeating cycle. It helped hide my real pain. But you can get very weary trying so, so hard, and not even realise why.[1]

I know that *I* didn't realize why. In fact, I came to understand the role of shame in my life almost by accident.

Looking behind the curtain

When I first started thinking about shame, I was more interested in other people's shame than my own. I was working as a missionary in Japan, trying to share the gospel with people who were culturally very different from me. I tried to talk to them about sin and forgiveness, but it just didn't seem to connect. I'd read that some missionaries had been framing the gospel in terms of saving face and avoiding shame, which are very important values in Japan. I noticed that when I tried this, I got a much more positive response. People's experience of shame provided a 'way in' to talking about what God had done for them.

After Japan, I taught church planting at a missionary training college. There's a lot of discussion about 'honour and shame' in the missionary world right now, so I began to explore those ideas with my colleagues. We soon realized that people were using the word 'shame' in a range of different ways, but nobody seemed to stop to ask, 'What *is* shame, really? Where does it come from? And how do we get rid of it?'

As I began to look more deeply into the different ways in which shame manifests itself, things became very personal, very quickly. The language of shame gave me a new vocabulary to express myself, a new way to understand why I was the way I was. I'd never once thought of myself as having a shame problem, but the more I read about the symptoms, the more the diagnosis seemed to fit!

I wonder if it's a man thing. Brené Brown says that men and women experience shame in similar ways, but our society forces men to operate out of a very limited emotional toolbox. One of the few emotions we feel comfortable calling upon is anger. When we're ashamed of ourselves we can often get angry, so we think that anger is the real problem. Or maybe we get defensive, so we think that defensiveness is the real problem. Shame can underpin so much of our lives, but because it often presents itself through another emotion, it can be very hard to detect. It lurks behind the curtain, whispering directions, while other emotions take centre stage. We can go through life without ever really realizing how much shame is affecting us.

What I want to do in this book is to help you to look behind the curtain and see what part shame plays in your life and the lives of those around you, and to give you the vocabulary to express it.

If you're like me and you discover that shame has affected the way you relate to the world, this might be a painful process. Shame forces us beyond sin management, beyond the idea that sin is something we *do*: 'I did this bad thing, and I should stop doing this bad thing.' Instead, shame confronts us with the reality that our sins come from who we *are*. There have been times on this journey that I have become more disgusted with myself as I have come to a deeper realization about what's behind some of my attitudes and behaviours.

But there's good news. As well as understanding shame, I want us to find grace for it and freedom from it. I know that Jesus came to free us not just from the burden of sin that we carry before God, but also from the burden of shame that we carry before the world. I know this, because he's done it for me.

At the same time, this freedom isn't just something for me and for you. We'll see that one way God heals a shamed person is by bringing them into relationship and community. If that's true, then, as the community of God, we *all* need to be equipped to talk about shame and to understand what shamed people are going through, and we all need to be able to show them the way out. My prayer for you is that, as you understand how shame works and what the Bible says about it, you'll be someone that God uses to bring grace and freedom to others held in its grip.

1

Feeling ashamed of my guilt

A young man is sent away to be expensively educated. Growing up away from the boundaries of his parents, he finds himself wandering away from God and falling into all kinds of temptations. Eventually he ends up being driven by pride, sexual lust, ambition, and 'by pleasing myself and by being ambitious to win human approval'.[1] Yet all the while he has a sense that God has not given up on him. He knows that God was 'always with me, mercifully punishing me, touching with a little bitter taste all my illicit pleasures'.[2] Looking back on his adolescence after being restored to faith, he writes about the overwhelming sense of shame he felt at breaking God's law.

This could have been my own story, but it is in fact a much older one: the *Confessions* of St Augustine, written nearly sixteen hundred years ago. As well as stories about sexual temptation and misspent youth, he writes of an incident when, as a teenager and goaded by his friends, he stole some pears. Reflecting on that time, he contemplates the nature of sin and how it affected him. He realizes that, although 'the theft itself was a nothing',[3] he stole purely out of a desire to do something wrong. He is less concerned with the fact of the theft and more with what it said about him as a person. This leads him to conclude that we all have an innate tendency towards sin from birth: Augustine's famous idea of original sin.

Yet what I find really interesting is that, as he thinks about the link between *what he did* and *who he is*, Augustine flips back and forth between seeing his sins in terms of guilt and in terms of shame:

> I went on my way headlong with such blindness that among my peer group I was ashamed not to be equally guilty of shameful behaviour when I heard them boasting of their sexual exploits . . . I was seeking not to gain anything by shameful means, but shame for its own sake . . .
>
> I would not have needed to inflame the itch of my cupidity through the excitement generated by sharing the guilt with others. What was my state of mind? It is quite certain that it was utterly shameful and a disgrace to me that I had it . . . As soon as the words are spoken 'Let us go and do it', one is ashamed not to be shameless.
>
> Who can untie this extremely twisted and tangled knot?[4]

We will try to untie some of the 'twisted and tangled knot' of shame and guilt in chapter 4, but this sense of feeling ashamed of guilt speaks powerfully to me. Like Augustine, I went through a wild time when I was younger. All through university, I struggled to keep hold of my faith, but I could not reconcile what I believed about God with the way I was living.

But, also like Augustine, I had the sense that God had a claim on me that he would not let go; that I was running away from him, and that I was not strong enough to turn myself around. The only Bible verse I could hold on to during those years was from Romans 7:15: 'I do not understand what I do. For what I want to do I do not do, but what I hate I do.'

What was worse, the shame that I felt made it harder for me to come back to church, even when I wanted to. I felt like damaged goods. And I didn't have any examples to draw on. I had heard many testimonies of people who had lived rebellious lives *before* they became Christians, but *after* they had come to faith? That wasn't supposed to happen. I felt like I knew what God had wanted and I had done the exact opposite.

Knowing that God could deal with my guilt was not enough for me. The *shame of my guilt* kept me – and, I suspect, keeps a great number of others – from coming back home.

All for Jesus?

I can't remember exactly how and when I surrendered to God again. I'm told that my church leaders had been praying for me. I vaguely remember long, late-night talks with some of them, times when they picked me up out of the gutter and tried to get me back on my feet. I look back in amazement at their patience with me.

When I finally summoned up the courage to come back to the church, a big step in my restoration came when the pastor's wife invited me to be involved in the children's church. To be honest, they were desperate for the help. But helping them in turn helped me. Perhaps a part of it was that explaining the truths of God to others in simple terms made me realize those truths myself again, but I think there was also something else going on. I was someone who needed to be needed. By giving me a way to be useful in the church, God was telling me that he had not finished with me; that, despite my feelings of shame and inadequacy, other people could rely on me again.

I wonder now if that desire to be useful may have been part of what led me to become a missionary. I certainly believe I heard God calling me to Japan, but, looking back, I realize that a lot of my own language around that call was about 'being useful', 'using my gifts' in the Japanese language, and so on. Like Augustine, I was still 'ambitious to win human approval'. If anything, I became *more* driven, more desperate to prove myself. For those of us who are insecure to begin with, Christian ministry can give us a way to legitimize our drivenness, to try to turn it into something positive. We can kid ourselves into thinking that we're giving our all for God's glory, when we're actually just trying to satisfy our need to achieve.

And so, by now in Japan, I worked exceptionally hard, sometimes preaching five sermons on a Sunday, running youth groups and home groups, planning evangelistic events and church plants into new areas . . . but why? For sure, I genuinely wanted the Japanese people to know God better – but I can't help wondering if, deep down, I wanted them to know God better *because of me*. Was I just trying to make myself look good in front of my congregation and my senior pastor?

Or was it that I was trying to make myself look good in front of God? To show *him* how hard I was working, and then maybe he would love me more? The problem was, after all I had done, I was pretty sure how God felt about me: disappointing. Embarrassing. Unlovable. Sure, he had forgiven me; but he was God. He had to.

I was starting to see how avoiding shame and 'saving face' were a big part of the lives of my Japanese friends, and how talking about these things could be a great way to introduce them to Jesus. But the more I told others about how God could help with their shame, the more I began to realize that I needed his help with my own.

Reports of shame's death are greatly exaggerated

I don't think I heard anything about shame in all my missionary training; in fact, I don't think I've ever heard any teaching on it in a church. It's something that doesn't quite fit into our Western understanding of Christianity – which is strange, because shame is something that affects every single one of us.

At the beginning of 2016, our family moved to another new country: this time to Australia. I was starting a new role as a teacher at a missionary training centre. We left our tiny, sixth-floor apartment in the middle of a huge city and moved on to a leafy college campus in rural Tasmania. Our lives changed completely. In Japan, we would get the lift down to the supermarket at the bottom of our tower block. In Australia, we would walk down to the farm and feed the pigs.

The change of culture, too, was a shock to the system. In Japan, there's a proverb that says, 'The nail that sticks up will be hammered down.' Life is dominated by the pressure to fit in, to be just like everyone else and not stand out from the crowd. Australia, on the other hand, is the most individualistic society on the planet.[5] You're *encouraged* to be different, to express yourself; everyone's *trying* to stand out from the crowd.

And so you would expect that Australia might *not* be the kind of place where you would find people wrestling with the burden of shame. Everyone is free to go their own way and to do their own thing, to be whoever they want to be. So I was shocked to see how often the shame dynamics I had noticed in Japan were just as prominent in Australia.

In May 2015, at Westfield Knox Shopping Centre in Victoria, a man took out his phone to take a selfie with a cardboard cutout of Darth Vader in front of a local cinema. His phone had both a rear camera and a front camera. Unfortunately, while the rear camera actually *was* pointing to himself giving Darth Vader a big hug, the front camera was pointed at some children. The children's mother, who was standing nearby, saw this strange man apparently taking a photo of her kids, and she freaked out. She took a photo of *him* taking a photo of her kids, which she then posted to Facebook, telling people to 'take a look at this creep'. At the end of her post, she said that the police had told her that if he was a registered sex offender he would be charged.

The post went viral. There were more than twenty thousand shares before the police were able to confirm his side of the story. By that time, the damage had been done. Hundreds of thousands of people had seen the post. The man's friends, his family and his employers were left wondering if he was a paedophile. He received death threats and felt scared to leave his house. As well as social media, the story was picked up by the press around the world: CBS News in the USA, and the *Daily Mail* in the UK.

Eventually, the man and the mother met and were able to apologize to each other. But before that, he told the *Mail*, 'We're a very strong, community-minded family and we've never had any issue with any form of impropriety and all of a sudden my name is smeared.'[6]

'My name is smeared.' If the way that we think about the world revolves around guilt and innocence, then this makes no sense. The man is innocent, he knows he's innocent and the police have publicly cleared his name. But even though he did not do anything wrong, his name – his reputation – is smeared. Even in individualistic Australia, we can't seem to escape the fact that the way other people see us matters.

When I talk about shame in the West – whether in Australia or in the UK – I tend to get two kinds of reactions. Some people will say that shame is dead. Looking at the way our politicians and celebrities behave when caught in a lie or an affair, they conclude that we are entering a more and more shame*less* society.[7] Others, like Roland Muller and Donald Capps, would argue the other way: that shame has become *more* prevalent. Capps writes that we have entered a 'narcissistic age', in which

> something has changed, perhaps radically, in the way that we today experience a sense of wrongness – wrongness in our inner selves, wrongness in our relations with other persons, wrongness in our relations with God. In our times, we are much more likely to experience this 'wrong-fulness' according to shame, rather than guilt dynamics.[8]

Muller lays the blame on Freud's theories of psychotherapy, which reduced the importance of personal guilt, and the slippery 'alternative facts' of politicians that militate against the taking of personal responsibility. If people no longer feel a sense of guilt, their sense of identity is derived not from inside them but from how they appear in front of others.[9]

How do we fit these two views together? To be honest, I am not sure that either is true. I don't think the *fact* of our shame has dramatically changed. From medieval public punishments to today's internet shaming, our society has always been motivated by shame. I think what *has* changed is that, now, different people are ashamed of different things from one another. When we had a fairly universal Christian morality, we might have all agreed that, say, lying in public is a shameful thing. But in today's post-Christian culture, we don't all have that same standard of morality. When we all believed the same thing about right and wrong, shame and guilt lined up along the same kinds of behaviours. But now they have become decoupled. We look at someone who blatantly lies and think, 'They should be ashamed of themselves.' It appears that they aren't ashamed of themselves, so we conclude that they're shameless, when actually they just don't share *our* sense of shame.

But, equally, we may not share *their* sense of shame. That same person who has no problem with being caught in a lie may be absolutely mortified at being the butt of a joke, which might be something that we could shrug off without a second thought. Shame is neither on the increase nor on the way out; it is still just as powerful as it always has been.

The shame that lingers

As Augustine continues his *Confessions*, he remembers how he found forgiveness in Christ for his sin and joy at the freedom from his guilt. But, despite all that, at the end of the book, we still do not get a sense that he is free from the shame of his guilt.

In Book X, 'Memory', he writes that he is still ashamed of who he is:

> Now, however, my groaning is witness that I am displeased with myself. You are radiant and give delight and are so an object of love and longing that I am ashamed of myself and reject myself.[10]

He finds that the memories of his past sins continue to trouble him:

> But in my memory of which I have spoken at length, there still live images of acts which were fixed there by my sexual habit. These images attack me. While I am awake they have no force, but in sleep they not only arouse pleasure but even elicit consent, and are very like the actual act. The illusory image within the soul has such force upon my flesh that false dreams have an effect on me when asleep, which the reality could not have when I am awake.[11]

And he wonders why God has not freed him from the power of these memories:

> It cannot be the case, almighty God, that your hand is not strong enough to cure all the sicknesses of my soul and, by a more abundant outflow of your grace, to extinguish the lascivious impulses of my sleep . . . It is no great matter for you to cause the impulse to give no pleasure at all or no more than can be checked at will in the chaste mind of a sleeping man, not merely in later life but at my present age. Nevertheless, I have now declared to my good Lord what is still my present condition in respect of this kind of evil. I 'exult with trembling' (Ps. 2:11) in what you have granted me, and grieve at my imperfect state.[12]

Once again, I can relate to what Augustine experienced. When I came back to church after university, I confessed and prayed through all the things that I had done. I knew that God had forgiven me completely. But I could still remember all the things that I had done, the times I had knowingly and deliberately betrayed God. What to do about the memories? What to do about the fact that I was *that kind of person*? The problem I had with my sin was not just its effect on God – Jesus had dealt with that – but also its effect on me.

In Heather Davis Nelson's book *Unashamed*, she writes that 'shame is what lingers even after I have confessed and repented of my sin'.[13] From God's perspective, forgiveness of guilt wipes the slate clean; but from our perspective, our feelings of shame over our guilt remain. They continue to torment us and to rupture our relationships with ourselves, with others and with God: 'Shame would insist that I continue to berate myself with the lies that I'm a bad wife for being impatient; that this is how I'll always be; that one day my husband will get fed up and stop loving me; that *God himself* is tired of forgiving me.'[14]

It took me many years to accept that God doesn't just grudgingly forgive me every time I mess up, but that he actually *likes* me, that he wants to be with me. That he is not ashamed of me.

And I'm sure I'm not the only one. How many of us can say that we have a right relationship with God, that we know we are free and forgiven and accepted by him – but we're still living with feelings of inadequacy, jealousy, failure and regret? We tell people that God loves them, and we hope that this will change the way they think about themselves. But without providing a path to minister grace and freedom for their shame, there's no guarantee that it will. That path is what we're going to develop in the rest of this book.

Over to you

At the end of each chapter, I'd like you to stop and reflect on some questions. Maybe you're not used to interacting with a book in this sort of way. But shame is a deeply personal thing, and I believe it's something that affects all of us. Each of us has a shame story. Our exploration of shame can't just be about increasing our understanding; understanding needs to lead to finding grace and freedom.

So take some time to listen to God as you prayerfully consider these questions. I believe you'll find there are things he wants to say to you about shame in your life, and things that he wants to do in you as a result.

- Have you felt stupid or embarrassed at any time during the past week? Looking further back into your life, are there certain events or experiences in the past that you feel ashamed of or embarrassed about when you remember them?
- Are there things in your life that you're still ashamed of at the moment?
- What is behind your shame? You might find that there are certain messages that you keep hearing when you feel ashamed: 'I'm such an idiot.' 'I'm just a fat slob.' 'If only I wasn't born like this.' When are the times that you most often hear the voice of shame talking? What does it say to you?

2

In the beginning

I want us to start our journey of understanding shame by looking at the story of the fall in Genesis 3. I think we'll find that this part of the Bible says a lot more about shame than we might have realized, and it will give us some hints about what God's solution to shame is going to look like. In particular, we're going to discover three important things about shame: *shame is everywhere, shame is horizontal* and *shame remains.*

We all know how the Bible starts: God makes the universe. God makes us. Everything is perfect: the man and his wife are both naked, and they feel no shame.

But then it all goes wrong:

When the woman saw that the fruit of the tree was good for food and pleasing to the eye, and also desirable for gaining wisdom, she took some and ate it. She also gave some to her husband, who was with her, and he ate it. Then the eyes of both of them were opened, and they realised that they were naked; so they sewed fig leaves together and made coverings for themselves.

Then the man and his wife heard the sound of the LORD God as he was walking in the garden in the cool of the day, and they hid from the LORD God among the trees of the garden. But the LORD God called to the man, 'Where are you?'

He answered, 'I heard you in the garden, and I was afraid because I was naked; so I hid.' . . .

The LORD God made garments of skin for Adam and his wife and clothed them.

(Genesis 3:6–10, 21)

We're going to see that the story of the fall starts and finishes with the theme of shame, and in the middle it talks about nakedness, fear, hiding away – all of which are tied up with the universal experience of shame. The only emotion that's really described in this story is shame.[1]

The story we don't know

I hope you'll forgive me if I don't spend much time in this chapter talking about guilt in Genesis. We're going to look at the relationship between shame and guilt in chapter 4, and, well, this *is* a book about shame.

More to the point, the guilt story is one we *already know.* God gave Adam and his wife a commandment. They broke the commandment. They sinned against him, and so, by any definition, they're guilty. We know how Jesus deals with our guilt, and we also know how guilt fits into the bigger picture of the Bible; Romans 5:12–18, for example, talks about how Adam's guilt brings death while Jesus' obedience brings life. But, as Timothy Tennent says:

If we only know about guilt, there is a danger toward legalism and a depersonalization of what it means to be a human in rebellion against God and in discord with our neighbour. If we only know about shame, there is a danger of losing the clear objective basis for God's righteous judgment that transcends the changing vagaries of human culture.[2]

So guilt and shame need to be held in tension. But Tennent also says that, in the West, we come with an expectation that the Bible is talking about guilt, and so we often miss the bits that talk about shame. We have to recognize the role of shame in these narratives so that we can 'be challenged to reflect more adequately the testimony of Scripture'.[3] In other words, let's go back to the Bible and look more closely at the parts of the story that we might have missed.

Chris Wright has shown how guilt and shame can live alongside one another. For him, understanding the place of shame in Genesis does not take away from what we know about guilt, but actually adds to it.[4]

But as we begin to see what Genesis says about shame, we will discover a story that we *don't* know. If you read commentaries on Genesis, you'll find that theologians often don't quite know what to do with the shame they find there. Gerhard von Rad, for example, mentions that shame is the first reaction that Adam and Eve have to their disobedience. But then he admits that he doesn't know why shame is brought into the story, calling it 'one of the most puzzling phenomena of our humanity'.[5] Klaus Westermann writes that the shame felt by Adam and Eve is 'something much broader and much more basic than what we call sin or guilt', but he too throws up his hands and calls it 'an extremely puzzling phenomenon'.[6]

So I would like us to take the guilt story, the story that we know, as read, and see if reading Genesis 3 with our 'shame glasses' on can give us some insight into the story that we don't know.

A shame sandwich

The book of Genesis starts with two accounts of how the world was made: one story runs from 1:1 to 2:3, and then there is a retelling in 2:4–24. Next, we've got the story of humanity's rebellion against God in Genesis 3. But I wonder if you've ever noticed the little verse in the middle, Genesis 2:25:

> The man and his wife were both naked, but they were not ashamed.[7]

We're between two stories here. The Bible has finished talking about creation and it's about to go on to talk about the fall. But right at that point, totally out of the blue, the author decides to mention the idea of shame.

Odd, isn't it? The Bible could have said they were both naked and didn't feel cold. Instead, we're told they were naked and didn't feel *ashamed*. By mentioning shame here, even to say that they *didn't* feel it, the narrator is dropping a hint that shame is a big part of what's coming next as we go on to read the rest of the story. The verb in the phrase 'were not ashamed' is open-ended; it talks about something that's been going on for a while. Randall Buth writes that 'the tense is used to provocatively present an open-ended stage for the following story of Genesis 3'.[8] Shame sets the scene for the fall.

Jumping ahead to the end of the story, Genesis 3:21 tells us, 'The LORD God made garments of skin for Adam and his wife and clothed them.' Nakedness and shame at the start; nakedness and shame covered at the end. In Hebrew stories, we often find that an idea at the start of the story is connected with an idea at the end, to form an envelope around the whole.

(It's a storytelling technique called an *inclusio*.) By putting the story into a shame sandwich, the Bible is making it clear that this is a story where nakedness and shame are dominant features.[9]

We can also see that the nakedness is a particular kind of nakedness. We can tell this because there's a lot of wordplay in Hebrew stories. Storytellers will use words that sound similar to make a connection between different ideas. This story plays with three very similar sounding words: naked (*'ārôm*), shrewd (*'ārûm*) and cursed (*'ārûr*).

> The Man and Woman are naked (*'ărûmmîm*) whereas the snake is sly (*'ārûm*) ... The pun continues when, expecting to open their eyes with new wisdom, they discover only that they are without clothing, simply naked (*'êrummim*).[10]

Finally, the very same snake (and only the snake) is cursed by God; it is *'ārûr* (Genesis 3:14).

The writer is using this wordplay to draw a line between the ideas of shame, nakedness, shrewdness and the curse.[11] There's a similar connection in English: our words 'shame' and 'skin' are linked, as they both come from the same Indo-European word *skam*, meaning 'hide', both as a verb (to run away and disappear) and as a noun (another word for skin). We hide our skin because of our shame.[12]

Why are these words being connected? I believe it shows us that when Genesis says that 'the man and his wife were both naked', this is not just a matter of *nudity* – the simple fact of not having any clothes on – but about *nakedness* – being exposed, vulnerable and ashamed.

Shame is everywhere

Shame doesn't just appear at the start and end of the story. It also turns up right in the middle:

> When the woman saw that the fruit of the tree was good for food and pleasing to the eye, and also desirable for gaining wisdom, she took some and ate it. She also gave some to her husband, who was with her, and he ate it.
>
> Then the eyes of both of them were opened, and they realised that they were naked; so they sewed fig leaves together and made coverings for themselves.
>
> Then the man and his wife heard the sound of the Lord God as he was walking in the garden in the cool of the day, and they hid from the Lord God among the trees of the garden.
>
> (Genesis 3:6–8)

When humanity first became aware of our rebellion against God, how did we react? First, there was the 'aha' moment. Our eyes were opened. We *realized* what we had got ourselves into. Next, we wanted to cover up. Finally, we needed to hide, to run away from the consequences of our action.

The narrator has warned us to be on the lookout for shame. And then this happens: realization, the wincing feeling when we discover that it's all gone wrong; covering up; wanting to disappear. Isn't this what it looks like when we're ashamed of ourselves?

The narrative does not take up the word 'shame', but the deliberate contrast between 3:7 and 2:25 suggests it immediately, and it is confirmed by the couple's behaviour. For what is shame other than a feeling of embarrassment which makes us hide?[13]

I've talked about 'our' reaction to the fall, because I see the story of Genesis as describing what it means to be human. The first emotion of the first person described in the Bible was one of shame.

> Man is ashamed of the loss of his unity with God and with other men. Shame and remorse are generally mistaken for one another. Man feels remorse when he has been at fault; and he feels shame because he lacks something. *Shame is more original than remorse.*[14]

I believe this is why the American Bible teacher Norman Kraus calls shame 'the primal moral instinct'.[15] If Adam and Eve first reacted to sin by experiencing shame, then so do we. Shame is a universal experience.

Shame is horizontal

It's helpful for us to realize that Genesis 3 describes two kinds of shame: the shame that Adam and Eve feel before God, and the shame they feel before one another. In both cases, shame changes the relationship. And the relationship that the Bible tells us about first is the human, *horizontal* one. We can tell this from Genesis 2:25. The story begins by telling us something about the horizontal relationship between the man and his wife. We have already seen that this verse sets the scene for the story; it tells us what we are supposed to look out for.

In many English translations, verse 25 reads something like this:

> The man and his wife were both naked, and they were not ashamed.

But things are a bit different in the Hebrew. Hebrew writers can put verbs into different forms to change their emphasis. The verb 'to be ashamed' here is in an unusual form, which is 'distributive and reciprocal (i.e. to one after the other, to each other)', and yet 'almost all translations ignore the implications'[16] of that form. If we wanted to really hammer out its meaning, we could translate it like this:

> The man and his wife were both naked, and each one of them was not ashamed in front of one another nor did they shame the other.

In the beginning, the man and his wife felt comfortable appearing naked before one another. When they didn't know they were naked, they weren't worried about how the other person saw them. There was no shame *between them*. Before the fall, they were naked but not ashamed; now they are naked and ashamed. Before the fall, they were united; now they are strangers to one another.

What's changed? It's not their nakedness; it's the way they see each other. What happened was that 'the eyes of both of them were opened'. They looked, they saw that they were naked, and they saw that someone else was looking at them. Being seen naked and exposed is terrifying for them. For Adam and Eve, 'shame is already the fear of the alien look'.[17] Psychologists have pointed out that shame is all about being seen by someone; having someone's eyes on us both unites us to and separates us from that person, and 'shame is "located" at the interface between these two qualities of the gaze'.[18]

Recently I was at a birthday party, and towards the end I was chatting with a friend. His wife had earlier mentioned that it had been her first day at a new job and she was looking forward to getting home. As I continued talking to him, his wife was urging their daughter out of the room, and I noticed that she was giving him The Look that signalled it was time for him to wrap up and go home. He hadn't seen her, and as long as he wasn't aware of her gaze, he was happily talking to me. Eventually I drew his attention to his wife's look, and he soon got the message to pack up and leave. What made the difference was being aware of the other person's gaze. Shame comes when we reflect on the fact that others are seeing us, and we begin to worry about what they are seeing.

As we begin to worry about what others are seeing, our first instinct is to try to cover up. At this point, we're not hiding from God, but we want to control *how* we are seen; we try to manipulate what other people see of us. 'The man and the woman are successful in hiding their nakedness from each other, but that does not exonerate them from the sin of their disobedience.'[19]

Let's remember that this is all happening before God arrives in the garden. This shame is something that first happens on the horizontal level, the human level. 'The threat springs *in particular* between the man and the woman.'[20] It is only later, in verse 8, that God enters the scene: first they hear him (they don't see him – that idea of the gaze again), and then they hide from him.

Even *after* God shows up, the Bible emphasizes the fact that shame has poisoned their horizontal relationship. 'The man and the woman avoid their responsibility by putting the blame on the other party. The man accuses his wife, showing that the wine of their love has turned sour.'[21]

Shame changes their vertical relationship with God as well, but perhaps not in the way that we might think. They've now become afraid of him, and they hide themselves away from him. But nowhere do we see *God* being ashamed of *them*. When we sin, we might feel emotionally that God *is* ashamed of us, and I know some people do use that as a way to explain the gospel. But this isn't how the Bible tells the story. Instead, God meets the man and his wife and talks to them in their place of shame, apparently without any embarrassment on his part. The problem he has with them is not their nakedness or their unacceptability, but the fact that they disobeyed him. So an explanation of the gospel in terms of a solution for shame can't make the problem of shame to be God's problem, as if somehow God lost face or was himself shamed by our disobedience.

Shame is relational and so it is *horizontal*, and it plays out first of all on the human horizon. As Claus Westermann puts it, 'shame originally is not something that takes place in the individual, but in relationship with others.'[22]

Shame remains

Shame is still a problem for us. Adam and Eve don't get their shame taken away. There's no solution to shame in Genesis.

At the close of Genesis 3, we see that God made garments of skin for Adam and Eve to clothe them. It's worth thinking about why he did that. They already *were* clothed. Weren't their fig-leaf coverings enough? In one sense, we can say that to get back in relationship with God, something had to die, for 'without the shedding of blood there is no forgiveness' (Hebrews 9:22). The ESV Study Bible notes say that the skinning of an animal sets the scene for the practice of animal sacrifices, which in turn sets the scene for the self-sacrifice of Christ.

But do *clothes* really help us to maintain a relationship with God? I don't think that can be it. The man and the woman were naked when God created them, and God declared them to be 'very good' (Genesis 1:31). God walked with them in the cool of the day, back when they were naked and felt no shame. So why does he now make clothes for them? Is God now suddenly offended by the naked human body? Of course not. God doesn't have a problem with our bodies, but he knows that *we* do.

> The last action of the creator towards his creature before expelling him from the garden is an action of care and concern . . . the creator protects his creature while putting them at a distance, and the protective action accompanies them on their way.[23]

So it appears that God didn't make garments of skin for his own benefit, to help himself out. It was a gift to them. They had needed to make clothes because of their shame and exposure before one another: they looked at each other, they realized they were naked, and so they made clothes out of fig leaves.

But why do they need *new* clothes? Well, there's a reason that not many shops sell fig-leaf skirts. The problem with fig leaves is that they're just not very *good*. They're thin; they break and tear; they flap in the breeze. God gives them a better set of clothes, clothes that are more durable, less see-through. He gives them these garments of skin to help them live with one another, because their shame problem is bigger than they can manage themselves. 'God does not compromise them in their nakedness before each other, but he himself covers them. God's activity keeps pace with man.'[24]

But while God gives them a way to be more comfortable around each other, he doesn't actually fix things for them. Clothes, even garments of skin, literally just *cover up* the problem. We're all still naked under our clothes. Take away the clothes, and we go back to scurrying for the bushes.

I think this already gives us a hint as to what real freedom from shame must look like. The answer to shame can't just be a covering. It is not just some kind of papering over the problem that allows us to go on living with one another but where shame comes back as soon as the lights go off. More and better clothes are not the answer.

Unfortunately, we *really* like coverings. Even today, covering up is the main way that we try to deal with our shame. I talked about how I tried to cover up my shame with achievement. We cover ourselves up with clothes, with money, with position, with honour and esteem. And, for a while, these might give us a way to make ourselves feel better or to score points with other people. But it's all just coverings. They might deal with the symptoms, but they don't actually cure the disease. 'The dialectic of concealment and exposure is only a sign of shame. Yet shame is not overcome by it; it is rather confirmed by it.'[25] Shame remains.

Of course it does, because the real root of our shame problem is that we're still surrounded by the gaze of other people, and we still worry about what they're seeing. As long as our eyes are opened to one another, we're in danger of being ashamed. It's that horizontal thing again: we don't really see ourselves as we are; we see ourselves as we think the other person sees us. 'Shame can be overcome only when the original unity is restored . . . through the restoration of fellowship with God and man.'[26]

We will only really experience freedom from shame when we give up on the idea of trying to cover it over. Instead, we have to learn to look in the right direction again. What I mean is that we have to learn to see ourselves the way God sees us. We need to get back to that state of getting our identity and our self-worth from what he thinks about us, not what those around us think. Salvation for shame means looking to him, and not to others, to be told who we really are.

Shame outside Eden

The Bible has given us three key insights to begin our journey of understanding shame. We've seen that shame is *everywhere*, shame is *horizontal* and shame *remains*. So what does this mean for us today?

First, I think we can say that if shame really is everywhere, and if von Rad is right that Adam and Eve 'do not react to the loss of their innocence with a spiritual consciousness of guilt; rather, they are afraid of their nakedness',[27] then this has to change the way we share the gospel. Genesis has given us a great point of contact with the world, a way in which we can speak into situations that people know that they are struggling with.

I mentioned that one of the things that first got me on to this journey of salvation for shame was my missionary experience in Japan. It's well known that trying to talk about the idea of personal sin with Japanese people is really hard. It's partly a language problem – the word used for sin, *tsumi*, means a crime such as murder or theft. So naturally people don't think that they're 'sinners'.

The thing is, I wonder if people in *Western* culture really think of themselves as sinners either. I'm not sure they do. We might need to explain to someone what it means to be a sinner, but we don't need to tell them what it means to be ashamed. They already know that. Shame is something we can tap into as we share the gospel, a common starting point we all understand.

I don't know about you, but the usual way I have heard of explaining the gospel begins with humanity's relationship with God. It goes something like this: you sinned; God sent Jesus to take your sin; he can forgive you. Recently, some evangelists, such as Sam Chan, have suggested that we can no longer assume that these ideas resonate in a post-Christian world. Instead, he suggests using shame and honour as a way in to the gospel story.[28]

But I don't think that this is just a matter of finding whatever works in our culture. We see all these themes of identity, acceptance and freedom from shame in Genesis 3, so it makes sense that they should be part of how we share the gospel. Shame isn't just something that's culturally relevant for today; it's actually right at the centre of the Genesis story.

Second, because Genesis describes both vertical *and* horizontal dimensions of shame, talking about the gospel as dealing with guilt and our standing before God isn't enough. While sin certainly ruined the relationship between humanity and God, there's more to the problem. At the end of Genesis 3, God explains the consequences of the fall, and those consequences remind us that sin also ruined the relationships we have with ourselves and with other people:

> To the woman he said,
> 'I will greatly increase your labor pains;
> with pain you will give birth to children.
> You will want to control your husband,
> but he will dominate you.'
> (Genesis 3:16, NET)

We need to show how these broken horizontal relationships are also dealt with by the good news of Jesus.

Finally, shame remains, because it's the result of a fundamental shift in how we see the world. Now that our eyes have been opened to one another, they cannot be closed again. This tells us why the world's ways of dealing with shame – hiding from it, covering it over – not only *don't* work, but *can't* work. When I experience guilt, I feel that what I've done is a problem. I can do something about that. But when I experience shame, I feel that *I* am the problem. And if I am the problem, I can't fix myself. I can only try to avoid the gaze of the other person, or cover over my failures.

But we know from Adam and Eve that coverings only deal with the symptoms. A permanent solution to the problem of shame is yet to come.

Over to you

I hope I've managed to demonstrate already that the Bible can help bring understanding to our experience of shame. We'll see that the Bible has much more to say about shame, and we'll also see that Jesus does provide us with a permanent way out of shame and into freedom.

Before we do, though, let's stop and think:

- When you talk with your friends and colleagues, what do you sense are their deepest needs and fears? Can you see ways in which shame might lie behind those feelings?
- We all have our preferred 'coverings' that we like to use to swat away our shame. As we saw in the last chapter, mine were success and achievement. As long as people notice what I'm doing, I'm OK. What about you? What coverings do you tend to use? How do you make yourself acceptable to others when you are worried about how they see you?

3

What is shame?

Tasmania is a fascinating place for a shame researcher to live. A huge number of the initial settlers were convicts, which historically was a source of shame but is now seen as a point of pride.[1] There's the disgrace of the 'Black War', which almost wiped out the Aboriginal population. And then there's the low-level stigma of being the butt of many years' worth of jokes from the mainland: the poor relations, inbred yokels with six fingers and two heads, and all that sort of thing. Tasmania is a place with a *lot* of shame.

You might not be able to tell that from the middle-class suburb we lived in. It's not a bad place, really. But when my friend Jo, a former missionary who now works as a midwife, decided to move out of her rented apartment and buy a house nearby, the only place she could get on to the property ladder was in the adjacent suburb. Sure, it was affordable, but for a reason: the area had recently been crowned by a reality TV show as 'the bogan capital of Australia'. (For non-Australians, think 'chavs', 'rednecks' or whatever your local social stereotype might be.)

Anyway, Jo and her family bought a house and moved in, and she went back to work at the hospital in the city centre. When her friends asked her how the move went and *where* she had moved to, she felt extremely uncomfortable; all she could say was, 'Just up the road.' She doesn't want her friends to find out her new address, although she knows that one day she will have to tell them. She's afraid that she doesn't quite fit in with her new neighbours, but she's also afraid of what her old friends will think of her when they find out where she lives now.

What's going on here? Jo is a strong, committed Christian. Unlike Adam and Eve, she's done nothing wrong. Her experience is very different from theirs. And yet we describe what they both feel with the same word: shame.

Four portraits of shame

This turns out to one of the biggest problems when we start to think about shame: it's a word that means all kinds of different things put together. One psychologist looked at a number of studies about shame and realized that they were all just talking past each other: 'All the discussions of shame in the literature . . . proceed on the implicit assumption that we know what we are talking about when we use the word shame.'[2] But do we really? I think it's more likely that shame is a kind of 'suitcase word', a word that 'we use to refer to many different mental activities, which don't have a single cause or origin'.[3]

What I want us to do in this chapter is to try to tease apart some of these different aspects of 'shame', and also to see what they have in common, so that we can understand how shame is expressed and what lies behind it. To help us do this, let's think about the following fictional examples:

Embarrassment: **Darren** is a teenager. One day, his mother walks into his bedroom to drop off some laundry, only to discover him masturbating over pictures of one of his male school friends. His parents had no idea that he might be gay. As it happens, Darren does not think he is gay, but he is going through a phase of experimenting with his sexuality. He stands up, rushes past her and runs out of the house. He never wants to see her again.

What's happening in this story? Darren experiences an overwhelming feeling of shame on being exposed. But he also feels ashamed at being misunderstood: his mother might now have an idea about who he is (that he's gay) that is different from his idea of who he is.

Someone else has seen him, and what she saw is not what he wanted her to see and not who he believes he is. He was discovered doing something that he and his family think is wrong, and this produced a sudden, powerful feeling of *embarrassment*.

Degradation: **Johnnie** is black. He has gone to the pub with a number of his white work colleagues, who are standing with him at the bar. It's his round, but when he tries to order he is told that the pub doesn't serve 'people like him'. Johnnie is angry at the way he is being treated. He can't believe people still think like that, but he also feels that it's *degrading* to be treated differently from them and that because of that treatment he doesn't get to have a drink with his mates. He's reminded of his blackness; he doesn't see himself as inferior, but he's ashamed that, because of it, he is receiving inferior treatment.

Johnnie is angry, but that's often how men react to shame. Underlying his anger, he feels that he has been *degraded*. Someone has looked down on him by some standard – the colour of his skin – even though he doesn't agree that this is an appropriate standard to measure people by. His experience of shame comes from the fact that a judgment has been made against him, and this judgment isolates him socially. He's been treated badly, and he's been made to look conspicuous and foolish in front of his friends. He's also been reminded that he has come up short against someone who has power over him. (Not much power, admittedly, but if the landlord doesn't like you, you don't get a drink.)

Once again, the reaction is immediate. His anger is a way of displacing and covering the shame that he feels. An emotional reaction again, but this time imposed on him from something outside, not inside, him. He's not disgusted with himself, as Darren is; he's disgusted that someone *else* is disgusted with him.

Disgrace: **James** wakes up in the morning and immediately remembers the disastrous job interview. Instantly, he's back in that meeting room, cringing in horror at the stupid things he said and how he felt completely out of his depth. He remembers how they actually laughed at his answers. In remembering, he *re-experiences the shame*, wondering how he could have been such an idiot. He screwed up his career that day.

The interview was fifteen years ago.

Once upon a time, James's shame feelings came from outside him – from his interviewers – but now they're internal; they come from within his own memory. We can see from this that it's possible to feel ashamed of yourself when there's nobody else around. Now, James's shame is not really about how he behaved at the time, but about his understanding of himself.

He was 'such an idiot' then, and he wonders if perhaps he still is.

The shame feelings James experienced fifteen years ago were never dealt with, and so that original shameful experience remains a powerful force many years afterwards. We're not talking here about an immediate emotional reaction; this is now a long-term mental *state* of shame.

Dishonour: **Debbie** grew up without knowing her father. Nobody in her family spoke about him, and she didn't know why. One day she discovers that, after racking up hundreds of thousands of pounds' worth of debt through a failed business, her father had taken his own life when she was two years old. The discovery profoundly affects the way she sees herself, and from then on she feels as if she bears the stigma of her family's past.

Debbie still talks about her feelings in terms of *shame*. But, unlike Johnnie and Darren, this isn't really an emotional *feeling* at all. It's not triggered by any particular event or memory. However, like James, Debbie's shame is something that she lives with, something experienced as a kind of relentless drumbeat in the background of her life, a long-term mental state of unworthiness, isolation or brokenness. Why? Because she worries that, if people were to discover the truth about her family, they would look down on her because of it. In fact, deep down she feels that somehow people can somehow *tell* her family history just by looking at her.

Debbie is ashamed to be seen because she doesn't want people to judge her on her family background, just as Jo was afraid to let others know her new address. Her shame is deep;

it is a matter of fundamental identity. It asks questions about her worth as a person. This loss of self-worth is more damaging than the kind of shame that Darren experiences, because it is a permanent state; the shame does not go away as long as her social condition does not change.

The shame matrix

Darren, Johnnie, James and Debbie have shown us some of the subtly different ways in which shame manifests itself.

We can see two *sources* of shame – where shame is coming from and how it starts. Darren's shame is internal, in the sense that it comes as a result of what he feels about himself and who he should be; James's shame was caused by something external, but it's become internalized. Johnnie's and Debbie's shame is external, because the shame is imposed by what other people feel about them – or what they fear that others feel about them.

We've also seen two *expressions* of shame – how the shame manifests itself in someone's life. There is a kind of immediate, powerfully emotional, short-term fight-or-flight reaction, the *feeling* of shame, in the case of Darren's situation and Johnnie's experience at the bar; and there's also a longer and much more damaging *state* of shame that Debbie and James experience, the pit-of-your-stomach feeling of dis-ease that never really goes away.

And so we can distinguish between at least four different understandings of the word 'shame', depending on where the experience of shame falls on the two dimensions of the *shame matrix* (see Table 1 overleaf).

These are my personal, preferred terms for these different shame experiences; I don't think you'll find them in common

Table 1 The shame matrix

	Feeling	*State*
External	Degradation	Dishonour
Internal	Embarrassment	Disgrace

use. I'm sure there are many more kinds of shame than just these, and many experiences of shame overlap more than one category. In fact, I think it's impossible to put a real-life shame experience into one of those neat boxes. But I've found that these terms help to give us a language to identify the different ways in which we experience shame. They remind us that shame is not just one thing, but a whole range of feelings and social consequences.

When I feel shame from an external source, there's a change in my social relationships and the way people see me: people look down on me – or I'm worried that they will. When it is internal, the more important aspect is how I feel about myself. There'll be some overlap, but we can see that, for example, Johnnie's shame is about how others see him but may not cause him to lose his own sense of self-worth, whereas the shame that James experienced fifteen years ago had a huge impact on his relationship with himself.

In some countries, such as the USA, being one of a racial minority can be a major source of external shame. Melissa Harris-Perry's book *Sister Citizen* talks about how society's stereotypes have forced African American women to carry around 'unwanted identities' which keep them bound up in shame.[4] Internal sources of shame can include mental and physical illness. People who are depressed can end up also becoming ashamed that they are 'so weak'. Those who have experienced sexual abuse or domestic violence can come to believe it was their own fault and feel ashamed that they 'let it happen', especially if people don't believe their story. These kinds of shame are so sensitive that I don't feel I can really do them justice by talking about them in a general way here, but they're important to be aware of. We will come back to look at sexual shame in chapter 10.

Some forms of shame can be short term – they can be easily dealt with and go away naturally over time. Other kinds of shame, as in James's and Debbie's examples, hang around for longer, and might well cause lasting damage unless they are dealt with. Other words that talk about different aspects of shame might include 'disgust', 'self-loathing' and 'humiliation'. Another word that expresses a long-term internal shame would be 'stigma', a word that came up in Debbie's case. I've chosen to label this as 'dishonour', because you might have heard people talking about 'honour and shame', and the shame that they mean there is a very specific kind of shame – a long-term, external state of being looked down on by others – and other experiences of shame can, in fact, be very different.

Seeing, judging and failing

So why do we give these very different experiences the same name: 'shame'? I believe there *is* a common factor. All of the things that we call 'shame' tend to involve three key elements: *seeing* or being seen, a *judgment* being made and *failing* to come up to scratch. Let's go back to the Bible and see how these three elements play into the Genesis story.

First, seeing and judging. We've seen that there's a theme of shame running through the fall account, but there's also another theme going on at the same time: the idea of seeing and being seen. Genesis 1 tells us seven times that God *sees* what he has made, and he *judges* it to be good (Genesis 1:4, 10, 12, 18, 21, 25, 31). God gives us a running commentary on his creation, 'a critical review' of his own work.[5] The Bible is establishing that there is a 'God's-eye view' of creation. God is the one we should be listening to about whether something is good or bad. And then God creates humanity, and this time his opinion is that it is 'very good' (Genesis 1:31). We are made in the *image* and *likeness* of God (Genesis 1:26). We're not just good; we're good because of our connection with God.

Then Adam and Eve look at each other. They're naked but they're not ashamed. There is no negative judgment. They see one other as God sees them. Something changes later and they *do* become ashamed, but for now, it's all good.

Next, there's the temptation, which is also all about seeing and making judgments. Eve '*saw* that the fruit of the tree was good for food' and finds that it is 'pleasing to the *eye*' (Genesis 3:6, emphasis mine). The serpent makes them a promise: 'For God knows that when you eat from it *your eyes will be opened*, and you will be like God, *knowing good and evil*' (Genesis 3:5, emphasis mine). The promise is that Eve will see clearly and be able to make judgments for herself, instead of relying on God.

And, as we know, that's exactly what happens. When Adam and Eve look at one other again after the fall, they start to judge each other. Instead of trusting in how God sees them, they make their own judgments on their own terms. Before, they were naked and not afraid. Now, they think of it as something shameful. They've lost that God's-eye view of the world.

And then what? How do Adam and Eve react to being seen by one another? The first thing they do is to try to manage and manipulate what the other person sees of them: covering their nakedness with fig leaves, trying to look more presentable. Of course, we know this feeling well. Isn't it exactly what we do on social media? We post holiday shots from perfect sandy beaches to show how exciting our lives are, witty and thought-provoking comments to show how smart we are, sweet pictures of how well our relationships are going. We see ourselves through the way others see us; we know that our friends are seeing and judging, so we make sure that what they see is exactly what we want them to see. This is something we're going to look at more in chapter 5.

So we see that the story of Adam and Eve has these three elements: they realize that they're being seen by the other, and that they're being judged by the other, and then they feel a failure because they didn't live up to that judgment. These three elements bring together all of the different experiences we've looked at under the common banner of 'shame'.

Defining shame

I'm not the first person to have tried to pin down exactly what shame is. Family psychologists Merle Fossum and Marilyn Mason describe shame as the 'sense of being completely diminished or insufficient as a person. It is the self judging the self.'[6] John Bradshaw is a family relationship counsellor, and he wrote about his own experience of shame, calling it 'a pervasive sense that I am flawed and defective as a human being'.[7] From a Christian perspective, I find Donald Capps' definition helpful. He's an American pastoral theologian, and says that shame is the feeling of being 'disgusted, disappointed or disillusioned with oneself'.[8]

I describe shame as the *feeling* and the *realization* that I am not acceptable, either to myself or to other people. It's a feeling because, well, we feel it. But it's a realization because shame isn't something we experience directly, like fear or anger. Shame happens when our brain jolts out of its ordinary 'getting on with life' mode and into a more reflective 'thinking about life' mode. This jolt might be caused by something that happens or something we do, or it might be an ongoing feeling in the back of our minds that we're unworthy, unacceptable or otherwise broken. So, to experience shame, a person needs to have a certain amount of self-awareness and self-reflection. We need to have the capacity to be 'consciously paying attention to ourselves'.[9] A 'shameless' person, on the other hand, is someone who just blazes through in 'getting on with life' mode, without stopping to reflect on who they are and how they're coming across to others.

I want to come back and look at the idea of 'the self judging the self', because it's worth thinking about what *kinds* of judgments we make. Often when we're ashamed, it's not because we're thinking, 'I did something bad.' It's not a moral judgment in that sense. When I'm ashamed, it's usually because I'm comparing who I think I am against what reality has shown about me. We all have a sense of the kind of person we 'really' are. Psychologists call it our 'ego ideal'. But we don't always live up to our ego ideal. There are times when we realize that we might not *really* be that person we think we are.

For example, my father was not a good husband to my mother. This formed a negative ego ideal for me: I don't want to be like that. And so a big part of my identity became that I wanted to be a good, reliable, faithful husband. But am I really? If I find myself having strong feelings towards a woman who's not my wife, I feel ashamed and disgusted. But the reason I'm disgusted with myself is not mainly because I think I've behaved immorally. I'm actually ashamed because my feelings for another woman have shown me that I'm not the person I think I should be. Shame is the nagging voice that says, 'You're a failure. You're no better than your father.' As we mentioned at the end of the previous chapter, shame doesn't say, 'I did something bad'; it says, 'I am a bad person.'

In fact, we can feel shame without any kind of moral judgment at all, if we fail to live up to really core components of our ego ideal. A really obvious core belief is that I can successfully navigate the fundamentals of life; to put it bluntly, I believe that I don't suck. What happens in reality? On the street, I see someone smiling and waving at me, so I smile and wave back. But he isn't! He's waving at the person behind me, and now I feel like everyone thinks I'm an idiot. They probably don't, but I feel like I've demonstrated to the world that I can't even handle basic personal interaction.

Shame is about the feeling of failing to be competently human. It is the realization of the fear that we might, after all, suck.

Over to you

- Look back on your experiences of shame that you identified in chapter 1, either recent ones or particularly powerful ones. What did they feel like, and how did you experience them? Where would you place them on the shame matrix?
- In those experiences, do you see common elements of an ego ideal that you failed to live up to?

4

Telling guilt from shame

In 2018, a huge scandal rocked Australia. It dominated the front pages of newspapers for days. It wasn't about politics, money or crime, but something much more important: cricket. Steve Smith, the Australian captain, had been discovered to have cheated during the third Test match against South Africa, by tampering with the ball.

Unlike the unfortunate man in chapter 1 with the badly timed selfie, this was a clear situation of wrongdoing, responsibility and guilt. What Steve Smith did was wrong. So why did the headline in *The Australian* newspaper that day read 'Smith's Shame'?[1] When do we talk about shame and when do we talk about guilt?

Let's take some time to think about the difference between shame and guilt, and what that difference means for us.

Quality, not quantity

We've already mentioned that shame is related to failing to match up to an image. It may be our own image of ourselves – our ego ideal – or it may be the image that someone else puts on us, whether or not we accept it for ourselves. People might say, 'Have you no shame?' if they want to tell us that we have failed to be the person *they* think we should be.

So shame is about values, and it's also about identity: who we are as a person. In the article about 'Smith's Shame', the

Australian Prime Minister was quoted as saying that 'our cricketers are role models and cricket is synonymous with fair play', while the head of the Australian Sports Commission said that 'this is about the values that Australian sport and Australian teams represent and stand for'.

'This is about values.' Steve Smith tampered with the ball, but that wasn't actually what people talked about. Again and again, what people emphasized was that he didn't represent the values that he was expected to. His 'shame' came from the fact that he did not live up to what it meant to be a good cricket captain, or a good Australian. It wasn't about what he did; it was about *who he was*.

Let's think for a moment about guilt, because guilt is a bit easier to understand. Guilt is what's called *deontological*, which basically means you can look in a rule book to see if it's there or not. There is a line, and I'm either on one side of that line or the other. If I cross the line, then I'm guilty. The speed camera doesn't care whether I was driving safely or recklessly; my driving was bad purely *because* it broke the rule.

In that sense, there's no such thing as 'slightly guilty'. We can talk about different degrees of what a person is guilty *of*. For example, we can say that murder is worse than manslaughter. But we can't say that murder is *more illegal* than manslaughter.[2] It's either 100% illegal, or it's nothing: 'For whoever keeps the whole law and yet stumbles at just one point is guilty of breaking all of it' (James 2:10).

Shame, however, has to do with values, and values tell us about *quality*. Rather than a bright line that we cross, there is a gradient that we fall somewhere on. Someone can be a good son or a bad son, or they can be a *terrible* son. This difference between quality and quantity, between values and norms, is why we sometimes feel shame and sometimes feel guilt. 'Shame assesses in negative value terms, whereas guilt assesses in negative deontological terms.'[3] Or, to put it another way, I feel guilty about breaking the speed limit, but I feel ashamed about my reverse parking.

We've seen that Adam and Eve first experienced their disobedience as shame. They realized that they were not who they should have been, and they felt exposed ('naked') for who they really were. They failed on the level of values and quality. And so do we; I believe that, like Augustine and his peers, we first experience our own sinfulness as a statement not about *what we have done*, but about *who we are*.

So shame is where it all starts. But later, both in the Bible and in our own personal understanding of God, we learn about the Law. This is when we move from an experience of God based on relationships and values to one based on rules. The arrival of the Law makes everything more black and white: I can relate to God deontologically; I can look to the list of rules and see if I'm on the right side of him or the wrong side of him. Some people divide the world into 'guilt cultures' and 'shame cultures', but if you look closely you will find that those labelled 'guilt cultures' are the places that have been most influenced by Old Testament Law and Protestant Christianity. In these parts of the world, we feel that God, like Father Christmas, sees everything we do and knows if we've been naughty or nice. Abiding by the Law turns us into a 'guilt culture'.

Because we start with shame and then move to guilt, we tend to get confused between the two. In fact, I believe that most of the time we talk about feeling guilty, we're actually describing shame experiences. This is most obvious when we're talking about sins against the self, rather than sins against others:

things such as gluttony, lust and so on. The classic example is the single woman who 'feels guilty' because she 'accidentally' ended up eating the whole tub of ice cream. (Or, in my case, the married man who scoffs the whole packet of Pringles.) That isn't guilt. What she is actually experiencing is shame. There is no verse in the Bible, nor does any country have a law, that condemns the eating of a pint of Häagen-Dazs in one sitting; there may not even be a family rule about who gets to eat how much ice cream. Guilt and transgression just aren't the right ways to talk about this.

And similarly, the man who pops but just can't stop is experiencing a sense of shame at his loss of self-control. He thinks that he's a self-controlled person, but reality has shown him that he isn't. He is ashamed because he has failed to demonstrate a positive value that he holds. In the same way, I might describe my questionable taste in 1980s disco music as a 'guilty pleasure' – but what I really mean is that I would feel *embarrassed* if anyone found out about it. Guilt language is often shame language in disguise.

Most of the time this doesn't matter. Who cares if I'm ashamed of my music collection or guilty of it? But if we can't tell the difference between the effects of guilt and shame in someone *else's* life, we can actually *really* mess things up. There's a very clear example of this that we can see in the Bible: the story of Job.[4]

Don't blame the victim

The idea behind the book of Job is to teach the Israelites the answer to the old question: why do bad things happen to good people? When life seems cruel and unfair, it's hard to accept that *things just happen*. Humans want to know that there's a reason for everything, so we tend to jump to simple conclusions: People get what they deserve. Bad deeds make bad *karma* which leads to bad results.

Let's have a look at what happens in Job. We start by being told that Job is a good man, and God is proud of him. God is so proud of Job that he shows Job off to the devil. 'Ah,' says the devil, 'take away all the nice things you've given him, and I bet you he won't be so devoted to you.'

'You're on,' says God, and he lets the devil bring disaster on Job.

Job loses everything: house, family, wealth, health. His friends see all this bad stuff happening to him and, from their understanding of how the world works, they conclude that if Job is going through a hard time, it must be because he has sinned.

And so they try to persuade him that he must have done something wrong, even if it was something he doesn't remember or realize. The only way they can understand his situation is as a punishment from God for his sin, and so, as night follows day, Job *must* be guilty of something: 'Who, being innocent, has ever perished?' (4:7); 'Surely God does not reject one who is blameless' (8:20); 'If he comes along and confines you in prison and convenes a court, who can oppose him?' (11:10).

'No,' says Job, 'really, I haven't done anything wrong!' And he hasn't. When the final verdict comes, God says that it's Job who has spoken rightly, and not his friends (42:7).

In reality, Job goes through a situation where he is clearly the victim. He ends up in a shameful state, losing his possessions, his status, his family and even control over his own physical body. He's finally reduced to sitting among the ashes of his old life, cutting himself with a crude blade to try to relieve the pain. But because they can only understand Job's situation through the lens of guilt, his friends end up making his situation worse.

But don't we do the same thing? I imagine we're more sensitive in how we go about it, but when our friends are struggling with issues of shame, identity, relationships or reputation, we can so easily try to turn them into spiritual problems. We're more comfortable with spiritual problems, problems that need to be solved on the vertical axis. We know what to do with them. If only that person had a right relationship with God, everything would be sorted out. Maybe there's some hidden sin they need to confess, and then the spiritual blockage of shame will be released.

But shame is not the same as guilt, and the solutions for shame are not the same as the solutions for guilt.

When a victim of abuse feels shame from her perpetrator, for instance, she does not first need instruction on how to confess her sin. She needs wisdom and courage to name the evil done against her as sin, and then to bring the lingering shame into the light of the beauty she is given through Jesus Christ.[5]

One of the things I've realized as I've been searching for a gospel that makes sense of shame is that not everything is a vertical problem and not everything is a spiritual problem. As well as dealing with the spiritual relationship between a person and God, we have to respond to breakdowns in the relationship that the person has with others, and the relationship that the person has with himself or herself. If we're going to take shame seriously, we need to know where guilt stops and where shame begins.

Shame contagion

We've already mentioned that guilt is about the action, whereas shame is about the whole person. Guilt says, 'Stop. What you are doing violates the standard,' but shame says, 'Stop. You are no good.'[6] Because of this, there's also a sense in which shame is contagious.

Let's suppose my son is at his friend's house, and I get a call from the friend's parents. The boys have been playing together outside; things turned rough, and my son has given his friend a good kicking. I might feel ashamed of my son's behaviour, because it reflects upon my own identity and values as a parent. There's even a word for this in German: *Fremdscham*, which means a kind of vicarious embarrassment. We can feel shame because of what other people have done.

There's a great example of *Fremdscham* in Judges 3. The Israelites attacked Eglon, king of Moab, while he was in his private rooms. Eglon's servants went to check on him and got no response, so they assumed he was on the toilet. They 'waited to the point of embarrassment' (verse 25) because it seemed like Eglon had been doing his business for an unusually long time. *His* behaviour made *them* feel ashamed.

But guilt can't do that. I can't feel 'guilty of' my son's bad behaviour. Guilt is individual, but the pollution of shame can spread through networks of relationships. It can even spread across generations. My German colleagues will tell me that, while they do not feel any *guilt* for Germany's actions during the Second World War, there is a feeling of collective *shame* even now. It's about values again: the war does not just reflect on those individuals, but it also reflects on what it means to be German. I wonder if, when God speaks about responding to

46

'the sin of the parents to the third and fourth generation' (Numbers 14:18), he's talking not about guilt, but rather about this kind of shame contagion.

The effect that shame has on us is much deeper than that of guilt, too. Donald Capps says that guilt is felt in the conscience, but shame is felt 'in the pit of the stomach'.[7] Shame is like a punch in the gut. We saw something of the contagious nature of shame when we looked at James remembering his past shame. Unless shame is completely dealt with, its power remains. When we remember a joyful event, it might make us smile, but we don't re-experience that same overwhelming sense of joy. But when we remember a shameful event, the gut punch comes back. We start asking those fundamental questions about ourselves all over again. Perhaps this, combined with the contagious nature of shame, is why we can find other people's shame really uncomfortable to watch. Shame itself is a shameful thing. Other people's embarrassment can disturb us in ways that stories of their pain or grief do not.

But while some of us find shame stories repulsive, others seem to enjoy this discomfort. In fact, there's a market for it. TV shows like *The Office* rely on the principle of *Fremdscham*, the cringe-inducing awkwardness of the shame of others.

The main character in the UK version of *The Office*, David Brent, genuinely believes that he's a sophisticated, successful and likeable boss. But, as viewers, we get to see what he's really like. *The Office* works on the principle of 'delayed shame'. We see the massive gap between David Brent's ego ideal and the reality of who he is, but he doesn't see it himself. Just like in a horror movie, when we know that the monster is in the basement long before the characters decide to look there, awkward TV keeps us feeling the tension of inevitable shame long before it arrives.

Shameproneness

I hate cringe TV shows. I find *The Office* skin-crawlingly unpleasant to watch, and I'd say the same about other portrayals of shame and awkwardness. My wife loves *The Apprentice*, another series that is all about the gap between ego ideal and reality; I just can't watch it. Why is it that some people love the shame of others and others hate it?

Perhaps one difference is that, while some people can watch David Brent and enjoy watching the idiot make a fool of himself, others have a kind of unconscious paranoia that they *are* David Brent. Deep down, they worry that, no matter how much they want to be respected, everybody around them thinks they're a sad joke and they're just too blind to see it for themselves. I think this is why those of us who are particularly sensitive to shame and judgment find these scenes of shaming others to be so confronting.

Psychologists describe this kind of sensitivity as being 'shame-prone' or having a 'shame attitude'. A person with a shame attitude is someone who's experienced a lot of shame over the course of their life but hasn't managed to dispose of it. They tend to see everything that happens to them through the lens of shame and the desire to avoid it. In James's case, I think the fact that he was not able to process and deal with his experiences transformed his short-term shame feelings into a long-term shameproneness.

We've already mentioned that we often choose between fight and flight as a response to shame. For people with a shame attitude, this colours the whole way we live: either we're running from the world or we're trying to take it on and beat it. On the one hand, 'shyness, humiliation, inferiority feelings and low self-esteem'[8] cause a situation in which 'a person's entire character can show severe constriction because he is constantly on guard against shame experiences';[9] on the other hand, 'conceit can be viewed as the opposite of shyness: it is an incessant, quite compulsive attempt to demonstrate "I must not be ashamed; just the contrary! Look how great I am!"'[10]

Remember my story? I chose to fight. My shameproneness worked itself out as a continual need to stand out from the crowd, to prove myself, and that led to me becoming arrogant and proud. In fact, a striving mentality can often be understood as a defence against shame; it's the intense need to beat the judgments of others, so that we don't get beaten by them.

Can God use our shame?

I've been talking about shame as something negative, something that we need to be free from. In most cases, it is. Shame is crippling and debilitating. Because it affects us so deeply, shame challenges us about who we are in ways that guilt does not. But the thing is, sometimes we *need* to be challenged.

Anand Giridharadas says that some kinds of problems are like engines that need to be fixed, whereas others are like crime scenes that need to be investigated.[11] When you're fixing an engine, you ask forward-looking questions, such as, 'What do I need to do to get this working again?' But for a crime scene, you have to ask backward-looking questions, such as, 'What happened here and why?' Guilt helps us to fix engines: I said something offensive, so I go and apologize, and the problem is dealt with. We can move forward. Shame, on the other hand, gives us a crime scene and forces us to investigate it. It makes us look backward: 'Why did I say that? What led up to it? Maybe I acted out of some need or insecurity in me. Maybe I *am* uncaring. Maybe something needs to change.'

I need to be careful how I say this, but I believe that, in *some* cases, and if we have the right attitude, there are ways in which shame can help us to be better. Shame is about how far I have fallen from my ideal, from who I want to be, the better version of myself. If I feel secure before God, then maybe I can filter out the messages that say that I'm worthless and hopeless, and take the time to see whether there is *some* truth in what shame is saying to me. Listening to our shame can draw us into a deeper place of reflection, where we can re-examine ourselves and begin to be different. 'Shame provides the primary foundation for conscience and for the instinctive sense of what is worthy or unworthy, right or wrong . . . Shame, in its positive influence, is the caretaker of our worthy selves and identities.'[12] I've learnt to listen to the voice of my shame. Carefully, obviously – not to agree with when it tells me how terrible I am, but to hear what it says about my character so that I can bring that to God.

In the Bible, too, I believe we can see some instances when God uses shame, rather than guilt, to convict people of sin. There are a number of examples in Scripture where public shaming helps people to see who they are and their need to change course. One such example is the story of King David and Nathan in 2 Samuel 12.[13]

David has been behaving badly. The armies of Israel are at war and his people are expecting him to lead them, but, instead, he's been kicking back in his palace in Jerusalem, checking out pretty girls. He asked his servant about Bathsheba, sent another servant to go and get her, and then sent yet another servant to get her husband killed. Then he brought her into the palace. So it doesn't look as though this affair is something that David is trying to hide; he doesn't seem at all *guilty* about what he's doing. Everything has been done in public, in the royal court.

Then, as now, royal scandals made good gossip. It's likely that everyone in Jerusalem knew what was going on, and David seemed to have no problem with them knowing.

Why? Because, according to the standards of his culture and his time, David isn't doing anything unusual. In our culture, we've got the rule of law. In England, we fought a civil war over the idea that even the king is under the law. It's hard for us to think outside of that culture. But the Old Testament world was not under the rule of law. If the king decides to take another man's wife and send him off to battle to be killed . . . well, he's the king, and that's what kings do. So as well as David feeling no guilt, we can say that he most likely feels no shame, because there is no gap between his behaviour and the expectations that people have of the king.

But God has different expectations, and he sends a prophet to remind David of them. Since this has all been happening in public, God gets Nathan to put the king to shame in a public showdown. How does he do it? It would be dangerous, even with the backing of God, to accuse the king directly. After all, the king is the law. Not even a prophet can tell him what to do.

So Nathan sets David up. He tells him a story about a rich farmer who steals a poor farmer's sheep. David is furious at the greedy farmer. But then, of course, Nathan turns the tables: 'You are the man!' David is shown up, in front of the whole palace, to be a hypocrite and a dishonourable king. It's this public shaming, not the quiet gnawing of a guilty conscience, that brings David to repentance. Maybe he actually does feel guilty when he comes to repent,[14] but it's certainly shame that gets him there.

Do I think we should go around publicly shaming people into repentance? No way. God is good at this, and he knows how to use our shame without crushing us. We're not. I certainly would not want to use shame to motivate people. Shame, especially our human shame, is almost always destructive. It's too dangerous a weapon for us to use, even with the best of intentions.

But I do think this should challenge the way we expect God to operate. He doesn't deal with everyone in the same way. Can we allow God to speak through feelings of shame, as well as through feelings of guilt? Perhaps some people won't come to realize their sin through the nagging of an introspective conscience; it may be that God works through their experiences of shame and embarrassment instead.

A bigger gospel

Why does this difference between guilt and shame matter? I believe the simple answer is that if we focus almost *entirely* on guilt, we sell the gospel short, and we don't deal with the entirety of problems that people have.

We so often restrict the good news just to the idea that Christ has taken the punishment for our guilt. But as I have tried to tell this good news to people in very different cultures, I have realized something important about myself. I could accept that God had forgiven my sin and taken away my guilt. But I still had to deal with the fact that I was *the kind of person who sins.*

God might not remember my sin, but I did, and it reminded me of my failure and my inadequacy. I was forgiven, but I still thought of myself as a pretty awful person. God dealing with my guilt was an important first step, but it could not be the end of the story for me. There had to be another step. If Jesus paid the penalty so I could have peace with God, what did I need to do to have peace with myself?

When it comes to evangelism, the difference between guilt and shame matters as well. I think we know how to present Jesus to someone who is wrestling with guilt. We have ways to share the gospel that can deal with that situation. But, as I've already mentioned, I don't really meet people wrestling with guilt. Both overseas and in my own culture, I'm much more likely to come across people who don't feel any kind of guilt before God, but who are really aware of their shame. A guilt-based gospel just doesn't scratch where they're itching.

Just like in the stories of Job and David, I don't think we need to convert people's shame experiences into guilt experiences to bring them to God. The Bible talks about shame, Genesis 3 talks about shame, Jesus talked about shame, so I believe we can talk about shame too. How do we do this? To answer that question, we've got to go beyond thinking about *what* shame is, and think more about *why* it is.

Over to you

- Think of someone you know who is going through a shame experience. What would grace and freedom look like for them?
- Think back to one of the experiences of shame you reflected on at the end of the last chapter, and bring it before God.

Ask him if there is anything he would like to say to you through or about that experience. Perhaps your shame has something valid to say to you, perhaps it is your ego ideal that needs to change, or perhaps the shame is irrational and destructive and needs to be healed. Maybe there's some combination of all three. He will let you know.

5

You are not your Facebook profile

In 2006, a Japanese psychologist described a new phenomenon he had begun to notice among his female students. While teaching psychology at Osaka Shoin Women's University, Makoto Natsume discovered that some of his students were getting depressed and falling ill – from smiling too much.

Young women in Japan are expected to smile all the time at work, and Natsume's students had been wearing these fake smiles for such a long time that their faces couldn't do anything else. In his book on 'Smile Mask' Syndrome,[1] he wrote that even when they were talking to him about problems in their lives, their faces formed the same unnatural smiles. After faking it for so long, they were unable to express their real emotions. As well as muscle aches and headaches, he found that constant smiling actually caused them serious psychological damage.

'Well, that's just *Japan*,' we might say. But have you looked at Instagram recently? Could it be that we're doing the same thing too – faking happiness until it drives us mad?

Digital fig leaves

I used to use social media before it was called 'social media'. Back in the 1990s there were mailing lists and newsgroups, and some people were beginning to play with something they called

55

'web logs'. I have many good friends that I first met online. Some of them I still haven't met in real life. So I'm not someone who thinks that internet communication isn't 'real' communication. It's all just people talking to other people.

But even I'd admit that there is something a bit strange and a bit dangerous about the way we're using social media today. I know that, if I'm not careful when I use it, it has a way of making me become boastful, proud, jealous or ambitious.

I want us to think a bit more about why this is. What is it about the online world that brings out the worst in us? My feeling is that the problem isn't actually with social media – what's happening online is a symptom of something bigger within us. In particular, it's about our *identity*. On social media, our friends only see what we let them see. We choose how we come across – and how we see ourselves. But at what cost? In her article 'Mistaken Identity', Ruth Ostrow writes:

> Watching my daughter grow up with social media, I can see that the whole construct of her online world is to make others jealous by being perfect, fantastic, having a wonderful social life, being popular and having fabulous bodies . . . These young adults get a false impression of the truth and live in a warped reality where mistakes, defects and vulnerabilities don't exist.[2]

We're using social media in the same way that Adam and Eve used fig leaves. Facebook and Instagram allow us to carefully construct an image of ourselves and then broadcast it to others. We airbrush away the hard stuff of life: the pain, the isolation, the insecurities, the failures and even just the mundane boring bits. We give the world a glowing picture of how successful we are, how content we are, how many friends we have. But it's not real.

The problem, of course, is that maintaining an image is enormously tiring, and maintaining an image of perfection even more so. When all our friends are involved in maintaining their own images of perfection too, we end up with a kind of digital arms race. We're all battling to constantly outdo one another as we try to portray a better and better life: more friends, more relationships, more experiences, more fun.

One student from Cambridge University wrote about this battle:

> I certainly feel the pressure to be perfect and it has got to the point where it's damaging my health. Social media is the main culprit. I had to delete my Instagram account because it would actually make me cry. I am a mature person with a firm grip on reality, but I have so many peers whose lives seem so perfect and sociable that it left me feeling worthless and lonely.[3]

I am sure the reason this causes us so many problems is *not* that we're lying to ourselves and deceiving ourselves. It's actually that we're too smart to believe our own lies. At some level, we know that the images we're portraying online are not the real us. When we're looking for the approval of others, we're not asking them to approve of who we really are, but showing them a manufactured impression of our lives that we think they would prefer to see.

And that's why social media gives us such a problem with shame. We've seen that shame is all about our insecurity with regard to how we're being seen and how we're being judged. So there's a strong link between our shame and the way we think about our identity. When we play these games with our social media profiles, we're widening the gap between our ego ideal and the boring reality; we're generating our own shame. We set ourselves up to fail, and we do fail, every time:

> Pressure to conform to whatever story we've created for ourselves doesn't come from highflying investors or an international audience: It's based in the simple fear of revealing yourself to be flawed and how the world (or just your friends and family – your world) will respond when you do.[4]

Identity curation

It's easy to think this is the fault of the medium. Social media gets the blame for our shame, as if it's doing something to us that's completely unprecedented. But I think we've seen that the desire to clothe ourselves in an image to impress our neighbours is as old as humanity itself.

I always wear a shirt when I'm teaching. I can't really explain why I do it; it just feels right. I'm sure that at my college it would be totally fine to lecture wearing a T-shirt. Some of the other lecturers do. But I just can't. I still find that wearing a shirt helps me to get into 'teacher mode'.

Clothes are an important tool that we all use to create an image for ourselves and to project that image to others. There's an entire global industry dedicated to giving us a massive choice over the image we want to project to the world.

For Adam and Eve, the first response to their eyes being opened was to make clothes. They covered themselves up. We mentioned in chapter 2 that this is something that happened before God appeared on the scene. And we do the same now. We want to control what others see of our lives. Ever since Adam, our defence against shame has been to try to manipulate the image of ourselves that we portray to others, a process I call *identity curation*.

Identity curation is something that we all learn as children. We discover that if we're seen to be kind and loving, people like us more; or maybe if we're seen to be funny and quirky, people like us more; or if we're seen to be brave and adventurous, people like us more. If we are seen to be 'good', we get a better response from our parents than if we show them our 'naughty' side. We learn to control what the world sees of us in order to get the reaction we want.

But, pretty soon, we confuse the image with the reality. In my case, I spent so long trying to impress others that my whole identity was bound up with what other people thought. I didn't have much sense of who *I* was any more. Like those Japanese university students, I couldn't be anything other than the mask I showed the world. Shame is so scary for us because it causes the mask to slip. It reminds that we're not who we say we are.

So in that sense, social media isn't doing anything different. It's just that it

provides an accelerated means of revealing our hearts. But it's not the fault of social media. The fault lies with how we use it and respond to what we see on it. We often use social media as a shield against our shame, but we always come up short because it isn't powerful enough to rescue us. And what we see via social media can trigger our shame in potent ways, resurrecting long-held insecurities and fears of exclusion.[5]

Social media sites are just tools. They allow us to project our image to others more efficiently, over greater distances and to more people at once. Instagram and Facebook are force multipliers for identity curation, but the problem of shame and identity has always been there.

West is guilt and East is shame?

Thinking about social media has shown us a serious problem in our world today: we just don't know who we really are any more. So who are we, actually? It turns out we always obtain our understanding of who we are from outside ourselves. Identity is *received*.

Roland Muller is a missionary in the Middle East who tried to work out what the gospel would look like for people suffering from dishonour shame. In his book *Honor and Shame*, he talks about the difference between 'guilt cultures' and 'shame cultures'. His idea is that in Western cultures, we put the individual first and so we're more guilt-based. In non-Western cultures, the group is more important than the individual, and shame is more prominent.[6]

But I'm not sure that's true. If shame is universal, then both Western *and* non-Western cultures are shame-based. Since Eden, we have always looked to those around us to understand who we are. I can't prove this, but I wonder if the difference is more about where we look *first* to find our identity.

Let's take an example. John is a young Korean man. He has grown up in a family and a society that sends strong messages about who he needs to be. He's spent his whole life picking up on these expectations: he's Korean; he's a member of the Kim family; his parents are doctors; he is expected to be a faithful son to his parents; it would be good if he grew up to be a doctor or something similar.

But John failed to pass the exams to get into medical school and instead got a job in a convenience store. He feels tremendous shame. Why? Because the expectations placed upon him by his society and family were very high, and he didn't live up to them.

But it isn't just because he failed to live up to the expectations of *others*. He accepted those expectations as part of his own identity and took them on for himself. If he hadn't agreed to what society demanded from him, he wouldn't feel shame. Of course, then he would have a different problem: if he were to refuse to go along with society's expectations, people around him would say that he 'has no shame'.

So in a culture where the group is more important, we first look around us to tell us who we should be. Society sets out its expectations of us, and we look inside ourselves and check whether we match up. If we don't, then we feel ashamed.

In the West, however, we have a really high view of the individual. We're a culture of 'I think therefore I am'. People tend to look inside themselves first, to try to work out what sort of person they want to be. We get to choose our own ego ideal. But there's a problem. Robert Albers says that 'more often than not, the identity which we find on our own is shame-based'.[7] What he means is that we're meant to receive an identity given to us by our natural families and the family of faith, an identity that tells us that we belong, that we are approved of. But when we try to find our own identity, we don't get the same satisfaction of knowing that approval – so we have to find it elsewhere.

Another example. Ed is a young British man. As he grows up, his parents encourage him to discover his passion and find his own way in life. They hope he'll go to university, but it's fine if he doesn't – as long as he's happy. He decides to be an architect, which is something new to his family. He falls in love and gets married. He and his wife decide to live in Edinburgh.

Ed has made a lot of major life decisions by himself. His family don't want to impose their views on him, but they want to support him in his decisions. They think it's all *fine*. But is it *good*? How does Ed know whether or not he's doing the right thing?

In a sense, Ed has the opposite problem to John Kim: when society is *not* telling him who he should be, he doesn't get the same sense of security about the path he chooses. To get that security, he'll try to find other people to validate his choices. In Stanley Grenz's words, 'the postmodern self looks to relationships for identity'.[8]

I believe it's a bit more subtle than that. We choose our own identity, but then we look around and find relationships that affirm what we've chosen. We might be individuals, but we're not islands: just like John Kim, if I do my own thing and don't care how society sees me, I might still be called 'shameless'. We need people around us to tell us that they approve of the choices we have made – and if they don't, we'll probably seek out new friends who do.

And it's not just about life choices. This insight about the desire to obtain validation for our identity has huge implications in the way we handle discussions about sexual orientation and gender dysphoria. As well as the surface-level discussions, there are often huge questions about identity and validation bubbling underneath. From the perspective of LGBT+ people, they have discovered something about their identity, and they feel the need to have their peers' stamp of validation and understanding on who they are. Often, however, they have found that churches or individual Christians have refused to engage with what they believe about themselves on a deep level.

But, in another sense, this is something that should be a point of contact. Gaining validation for our identity is a universal desire, regardless of sexual orientation or gender identity. It's not enough for any of us to just *be* who we are; we also feel a need for others to recognize and agree with who we think we are. Unless we engage with the underlying identity and validation issues, we're not going to make any headway on anything else.

So the difference between the West and the rest isn't just a matter of guilt versus shame. It's how we find our sense of who we are: either from within ourselves which is then validated by the group, or from the group which we then validate ourselves.[9] The problem, really, is that we are looking across to the world, and not up to our Maker.

What about looking in?

Brené Brown is one of the most popular writers on the topic of shame right now. She's done a lot of really important work, particularly on understanding the reasons why women feel shame. Her books have helped many people to break free from the expectations of others which they had taken on. For her, one of the keys to overcoming shame is experiencing empathy: to be told that you are OK, that someone else understands that what you feel is normal and acceptable, and that you don't actually disgust other people after all. When someone else knows your fears and failures and still accepts you, the power of shame is taken away.

But before you can experience that empathy and that acceptance, you need to be able to communicate your shame and fear openly with another person. Suppose you feel like a bad wife or mother because you can't keep your house as neat and tidy as you think you should. Nobody's going to tell you that your worries are totally normal or your expectations are too high, unless they know that that's what you're worried about. So experiencing empathy requires the courage and the ability to be vulnerable with others. The problem is that it's really hard to talk to people about something you're ashamed of.

In her second book on shame, *The Gifts of Imperfection*, Brown develops the idea that freedom from the judgment of others comes through practising deliberate authenticity: 'the daily practice of letting go of who we think we're supposed to be and embracing who we are'.[10] When we look in to ourselves and find our identity sufficient, then we don't need others to tell us we're OK. We can say to ourselves, in her words, 'I am enough.'[11]

Another way she suggests to build resilience against shame is to have compassion for ourselves. This is something that the psychologist Paul Gilbert also sees as a way out of shame: 'Learning to replace shame and self-criticism with compassion and compassionate understanding is important and will help you move forward in life and develop your courage.'[12]

Self-compassion sounds great; it sounds like grace. But does it *work*? I don't think so; at least, I don't think we can accept it as the final destination for the shamed. To understand why not, we've got to go back once again to where shame began.

In whose image?

When the serpent tempts Adam and Eve, his bargain is that they can 'be like God'. But hang on a minute. We've been told that Adam and Eve were made in God's likeness and image. They're *already* like God. So what's the offer here, really? We said in chapter 3 that by being able to tell right and wrong *without God*, Adam and Eve started to make judgments – about themselves, about each other – that previously had been God's to make.

We're *meant* to get our identity by looking up to God, not from those around us, or even by looking inside ourselves. Calvin's *Institutes* begins by saying 'that man never attains to a true self-knowledge until he has previously contemplated the face of God, and come down after such contemplation to look into himself'.[13] As we look upward to God, and hear his voice speaking out his evaluation of us – created 'in our image, in our likeness', 'very good' (Genesis 1:26, 31) – we get our true identity from him.

But once our 'eyes . . . were opened' (Genesis 3:7) and we realized that we were being seen by others, we started to allow other people to define us. Eve saw Adam and became aware of what he might be thinking about her; Adam saw Eve and became aware of what she might be thinking about him. And now this is how we live: instead of looking up and getting our identity based on what God thinks of us, we look around and worry about what those around us think. 'Having made their declaration of independence from God, they are now aware of themselves in a new way, as autonomous beings over against other selves.'[14]

After the fall, the story continues in a bit of an odd way. In Genesis 5, we're given a recap of Adam's creation: 'When God created mankind, he made them in the likeness of God' (Genesis 5:1). After the shame of Eden and the disaster of Cain and Abel, the Bible is reminding us who we are meant to be: 'So God created mankind in his own image, in the image of God he created them' (Genesis 1:27)

But next there is a sudden switch: 'When Adam had lived 130 years, he had a son in *his* own likeness, in *his* own image' (5:3, emphasis mine). I don't believe that switch is an accident; I believe the Bible must be making a point here. After Adam's eyes were opened, something happened to humanity which changed where we get our likeness and image from. I'm not saying that the image of God has been totally lost. The Bible, particularly in 2 Corinthians 3:18 and James 3:9, talks about all humans having been created in the image of God. But something has changed. 'Man is ashamed because he has lost something which is essential to his original character.'[15] We still bear the image of God, but now we are 'one step removed . . . Seth and his heirs are a strange unresolved mixture of the *regal* image of God and the *threatened* image of Adam'.[16]

Augustine said that we inherit Adam and Eve's original sin, but perhaps there's a sense in which we also suffer from original shame. When the human race turned its back on God, the link was severed. The nature of humanity has changed, and even now we can't avoid seeing ourselves through others' eyes, instead of through God's. Either we end up completely shameless, not caring what other people think of us and struggling to relate meaningfully to them, or we're bound up by the expectations of our family, our friends and our society.

This is why I believe that vulnerability and empathy can't be enough to solve our identity problem. 'A gap in Brown's research is the definition of humans as made in God's image, a concept termed *imago dei*.'[17] Brené Brown and Paul Gilbert want to free us from the judgment of others, but they do this by encouraging us to put our trust in our own judgment of ourselves instead. I admit this is better than being ashamed, but it doesn't go far enough. Stephen Gaukroger once compared agnosticism to a railway tunnel – a useful place to pass through but a terrible destination – and I think that's what I'd say about vulnerability and empathy. Instead of looking across, we now look in. But we still don't look up.

It's this failure to look up that is at the root of our shame. Shame is actually the *symptom* of a mis-derived identity. The experience of shame itself tells us that we're looking in the wrong place to learn who we are. We need to remember how to see. And that's something Jesus taught us how to do.

Over to you

- Think about some of the ways that you engage in identity curation. How do you make yourself look good in front of others? What would happen if you stopped?
- Why do you think people are so concerned with the approval of others? What are some of the things that stop them listening to what God is saying about them?

6

Jesus and shame

Jesus spent his whole life dealing with shame. His society was one where dishonour shame was a powerful force. Everyone knew what it meant to be good, what it meant to be holy and pure, what it meant to be respectable.

People who weren't any of those things lived in a state of shame. But these were the people who were drawn to Jesus. They knew he was someone who didn't care about what he was supposed to think of them. He wasn't afraid to enter into the world of the shamed and live alongside them. In fact, the reason the good, religious people didn't like Jesus was that he spent his time with people who should have been 'beneath' him. Wherever he went, Jesus displayed a scandalous grace: he scorned shame, turned it upside down and redefined it.

I want us to think about how Jesus ministered to people in shameful situations, to see what clues we can get from his example. We'll also look at what he taught his disciples about shame, and see how his life and death overturned the whole shame system.

Drinking with the enemy

Let's begin with one of the many stories about Jesus meeting a woman living in shame: the story of the Samaritan woman at the well in John 4.

Jesus has been travelling through Samaria, and he's hot and thirsty. He comes into a town and sits down by the well, at noon. A woman comes along to the well. She comes on her own, at the hottest part of the day. This is already suspicious; in the Middle East, women try to avoid the heat of the day, and they normally go to the well in groups so they can avoid any accusations of improper behaviour.[1] Why is she behaving like this? Perhaps it's because she has noticed the arrival of a lone, male stranger and is wondering where an encounter might lead; maybe she's not welcome among the other women. Either way, things don't look good for her. We gather, from what Jesus says to her later, that she's known for being promiscuous. She would be living her life in a state of social shame and disgrace.

But then, Jesus' behaviour isn't exactly normal either. If someone were to come out of their house at that moment, they'd catch a Jewish rabbi sitting alone with a notorious woman. Jesus, as a good Middle Eastern Jew, knows that this would destroy his reputation. We know it is a shocking thing to do, because his disciples *do* catch him and they *are* shocked! But Jesus doesn't care how the world sees him. He is so completely secure in his identity before his Father that his public reputation just isn't important to him at all.

In fact, Jesus breaks even more rules. He doesn't just spend time alone with this woman, but he also has a conversation with her. Jewish men wouldn't talk with Samaritans, and certainly not Samaritan women; yet here Jesus is treating her as an equal. By asking her for a drink when he has no bucket (verses 7 and 11), he's asking her to lend him hers. He makes her useful and puts her in the position of being able to help another person.

A shamed person feels broken, isolated and useless to anyone; Jesus gives her power, a role to play and genuine human interaction. And it really is a deep interaction, not just chit-chat – they have a political and theological conversation about the difference between Jews and Samaritans. Jesus seems to genuinely respect her views and her intellect.

Next, he has something to offer to her: he talks about giving her wonderful water that will satisfy her forever. She'd be glad never to be thirsty again, but it seems like she'd be even happier if she didn't have to make her lonely, shameful journey to the well every day (verse 15).

But then Jesus speaks directly into her situation of shame. She's been married five times and is now living 'in sin'. He shows her that he knows who she really is, and also that it doesn't matter to him. He gives her authority and status and commissions her to be his witness to her town. She will bring many people to faith in him. What she has done in the past doesn't make her less worthy before God, nor does it stop God from working through her in the future.

When I was in my twenties, one of my biggest fears was that I had blown it before God. Because of some bad decisions I'd made, I felt isolated from God's people and that I would just about scrape into heaven 'as one escaping through the flames' (1 Corinthians 3:15). I was ashamed of my past, and felt like I was no use to God any more.

Seeing the way Jesus deals with the Samaritan woman gives me hope. It reminds me that Jesus sees past the shame and isolation, and is always ready with a new challenge and a new commission. Even those whom the world writes off, he never writes off. His living water is still available, even to me.

He lifted me out of the mud and mire

Jesus also rescues people when others try to use shame as a weapon against them. We'll look at one example of this in Luke 7:36–50, where shame is used as a weapon both against the woman with the alabaster jar and against Jesus himself.

Jesus has been invited to dinner by Simon the Pharisee. Simon calls Jesus 'teacher', which means he's aware that he's hosting a special guest, and that in turn means there are a few rules he needs to follow. The first thing you do when hosting someone special is to greet them with a kiss. Then, you make sure your guest has washed their feet. Finally, you offer them some olive oil so they can wash and freshen up before the meal.[2]

Simon does none of these things. He calls Jesus a religious teacher, but Simon's actions show disrespect for Jesus and for his message. What would you do if you went to someone's house for dinner and they barely acknowledged your presence? It would be awkward at best; you might feel too angry to stay but find it too embarrassing to leave. Jesus says nothing, and simply takes his place at the table.

And then a woman comes into the room. The first thing Luke tells us about her is that she's a sinner. That's a pretty harsh way to identify someone. But it's also the first thing Simon thinks about her: she is a sinner. She's probably well known in the town to be engaged in some kind of sexual sin, either as a prostitute or as an adulteress. She lives her life in shame.

As we saw in chapter 4, shame is contagious. The stigma of this woman was so strong that no self-respecting person would allow her anywhere near them – certainly not a rabbi! From Simon's perspective, Jesus can't really be a man of God if he lets *someone like that* touch him.

But Jesus turns her shame on its head. He demonstrates to Simon that not only does he know all about her life and about her shameful situation, but he also accepts her in spite of it. Jesus declares that, regardless of her shame, *she* is the one that God has forgiven. She has treated Jesus rightly, with the love and hospitality that Simon failed to provide. She has provided a kiss of greeting, her tears to wash his feet and oil to anoint him: the three things a host would be expected to do.

Then Jesus turns to Simon and deals with his shaming behaviour. Using shame as a weapon can be a dominance game, but it only works if the victim continues to play the role of victim.[3] Jesus names the elephant in the room: 'You did not give me any water for my feet . . . You did not give me a kiss . . . You did not put oil on my head.' He calls Simon out in public for his disrespectful behaviour. He's saying, 'I see what you are trying to do, but I refuse to take the part you have planned for me.'

Next, he turns the crowd's attention away from the shamed woman and on to himself. When he says, 'Your sins are forgiven' (verse 48), suddenly everyone is talking about how outrageous his behaviour is, instead of hers, and she's able to 'go in peace' (verse 50). We often see Jesus as our substitute for guilt, but I believe we can also see him as our substitute for shame – taking our shame on himself so we can be free from it.

Here's how Jesus *could* have handled this if he had remained within the shame system:

It would have been easy for Jesus to have responded to the woman's actions with embarrassment, and to have taken such embarrassment out on her. He could easily have shamed her, using any one of the defensive strategies that we have at our disposal in such situations. He could have been contemptuous of her, treating her as the sinful woman that she was, knowing that no one in the company would have dared speak up if he had chosen to humiliate her . . .

That he did none of these things, but allowed her to carry out her simple, heartfelt ceremony is testimony . . . to the fact that he was ushering in a new age of self-other relationships, having a new set of rules, a new set of assumptions. [4]

Jesus' 'new set of rules' applies every time he interacts with someone. He sees them not in the way the world sees them, but as God sees them. He calls Levi, a tax collector, and makes him a rabbi's disciple (Luke 5:27); he publicly honours the Roman centurion, saying that his faith is greater than that of Israel (Luke 7:9); he gives the demon-possessed man identity and commissions him to evangelize his neighbourhood (Mark 5:19); he heals a crippled woman and hails her as a 'daughter of Abraham' (Luke 13:16). Bringing grace and freedom from shame starts with seeing the image of God in others and rejecting the judgments of the world.

The upside-down kingdom

The second way in which Jesus brings freedom is through his teaching. I was surprised when I realized how much of Jesus' teaching has to do with the way in which the world's shame system operates. So much of what he says is about the way we make judgments of one another, and about our desire to curate our identities to impress others and gain their approval.

First, Jesus overturns our ideas about what is impressive. While the world finds value and worth in sophistication, Jesus tells us we have to be like children (Matthew 11:25). Children weren't worth anything in the ancient world, but Jesus says they are the true owners of the kingdom of heaven (Matthew 19:14) and that the way that we treat them reflects the way we treat Jesus (Matthew 18:5). What does it mean to be like a child as we accept the kingdom of God? I think part of it has to do with coming before God without pretence. Little children don't try to be something they're not in order to impress others.

We're impressed by power and authority, but the impressive people in the kingdom of heaven are those who serve, sacrifice and suffer (Matthew 20:20–28). We're impressed by wealth and riches, but they make it harder to enter the kingdom; instead, if you give up material possessions, God considers you wealthy (Matthew 19:23–29).

Basically, says Jesus, we've got it all backwards. People who we consider to be most impressive in terms of status and power don't impress God at all, and those who have no status here on earth are counted as the closest to him (Matthew 19:30). The images of wealth, success, power and status that we curate and portray to others might score us a few points in the short term, but they're not what God is interested in.

Rules for shame-free living

The real pinnacle of Jesus' teaching about the shame system comes in Matthew 5 – 6, the Sermon on the Mount. Jerome Neyrey's commentary shows how the three sections of this sermon work together to overturn our ideas of worth and identity.[5] Jesus is teaching us to reject the shame system and instead to treat each other according to the image of God.

In the first part of his sermon, the Beatitudes, Jesus deals with the fact that being one of his disciples would be a shameful experience. The fourth beatitude, especially in Luke's version, really resonates with those who suffer from shame:

> Blessed are you when people hate you,
> when they exclude you and insult you
> and reject your name as evil,
> because of the Son of Man.
> (Luke 6:22)

Followers of Jesus in the first century would be shut out from the Jewish community. They may be thrown out of their homes and their families. We might know a bit about what it's like to be 'hated', 'excluded', 'insulted' and 'rejected', but in their society, losing family, friends and community made you a nobody.

Jesus' teaching is designed to give his disciples a way to process their shame. Yes, says Jesus, others may cast you out, disown you and make you feel like nothing, but I want you to remember that this is because you're on *my* side.

A 'strong man'

Next, Jesus blesses the meek. What does he mean by that? Neyrey says that Jesus is talking about how his disciples are to reject society's expectations of masculinity.[6] We'll see that Jesus expects them to forgive others, let go of wrongs, not rise to challenges, not defend their reputations or assert their own rights: the complete opposite of what it means to be a man in the eyes of their society. They would look effeminate, strange and weak.

Brené Brown says that men and women experience shame differently; for men, shame tends to happen when other men 'see anything that can be perceived as weakness'.[7] But no, says Jesus; meekness is not the same as weakness. It's not weak to *choose* to give way to others. It's not weak to *choose* to lay down your rights and serve another person. Meekness *is* an expression of strength, but it's strength that is channelled and directed into serving others. It's a different kind of strength from the world's strength.

I still don't think we've really got our heads around this. One of my church members in Australia told me that he found that the way I look and act as a 'scrawny little Pom' was confronting to his understanding of masculinity. Australians definitely have a clear understanding of what a man is meant to look like – and it basically doesn't look like me. Even in the churches, I would hear people talk about wanting to be (or wanting to find) a 'strong man of God'. But when you probe a bit to understand what they mean by that, it turns out that what it means to be a 'strong man of God' isn't really any different from what it means to be a strong Australian man: tough, uncompromising, decisive, independent and all the rest of it.

Jesus expects godly strength to be very different from the world's strength, and he expects it to be expressed in a very different way. 'Strength is creative when it expresses itself by making the weak strong.'[8]

Giving up the reputation game

Next, Jesus moves to laying out the rules for his new community. In a culture where men are expected to behave aggressively and to jostle for position over others, Jesus tells them to stay out of it; you're not allowed to try to get one over other people. When someone makes you angry, don't insult them (Matthew 5:22). If someone is offended by you, take it back and become equals with them again (Matthew 5:24). If someone is trying to use the law courts to attack you, make peace with them (Matthew 5:25). This stuff may be cultural, but it's also true today: Jesus does not allow us to play shame and identity games to score points off other people.

Next, when Jesus tells us not to swear an oath, he is talking about how people would try to defend themselves when their reputations were challenged.

> Men may not take oaths at all, and so they may not challenge others or defend themselves with them. Nor may they claim honour and status by posturing before their neighbors and swearing in verbose and grandiloquent ways so characteristic of peoples of the Mediterranean.[9]

For Jesus, our reputation is not a fig leaf that we should cling to, but something we should be ready to give up at any point. Jesus doesn't allow us to defend our reputations *at all*. We're not allowed to seek revenge on others (Matthew 5:39); we can't hold tightly to our property (Matthew 5:40); and we mustn't resist powerful people when they use their power against us (Matthew 5:41). We're not allowed to score points off others, but we're also not allowed to defend ourselves when people are trying to score points off us.

Finally, in Matthew 6, Jesus moves to 'vacating the playing field'.[10] It's not that we play the shame game by different rules; we simply don't play at all. Jesus expects his disciples to turn their backs completely on the world's systems of honour, prestige and identity curation.

Nor can we use the world's tools to make a name for ourselves. Jesus tells us not to 'display your righteousness merely to be seen by people', as the New English Translation puts it (Matthew 6:1). When we give, we should do it secretly; when we pray, we should do it simply and not to impress. Jesus is showing us a way of living that completely gives up on the idea of seeking glory and honour. Instead, he invites us to be satisfied with the name he gives to us:

> Jesus invites disciples to join his honourable world, where the opinions of neighbors do not count for much and where their expectations do not control one's behavior . . . Jesus' subversive commands would not be imaginable to disciples unless an alternative structure for worth, reputation, and respect were put in place, namely, honor from Jesus and rewards from one's heavenly Father.[11]

Doesn't that sound like good news for the shamed?

The cross of honour

Jesus gave people grace and freedom from their shame, and he taught his followers how to live in freedom. But Jesus did one more thing to show up the emptiness of the shame system: he died.

Jesus' main enemies were the Pharisees. I wonder if one of the reasons for this was that, as the religious leaders, they *should* have been the people who were most free from shame games. As it was, they played the shame game more competitively than anyone else. Jesus showed up their hypocrisy in the way they used an image of holiness to try to influence the people around them.

Time and time again, the Pharisees tried to win the crowd and to discredit Jesus, and each time Jesus got the better of them. Eventually they decided that they'd had enough of being humiliated, and 'began looking for a way to kill him, for they feared him, because the whole crowd was amazed at his teaching' (Mark 11:18).

But killing Jesus was not enough. They needed to reassert their dominance and their prestige. They didn't want just to kill him, but to humiliate him utterly. Crucifixion would be the perfect solution.

> The cross was designed above all to be an instrument of contempt and public ridicule. Crucifixion was the most shameful treatment execution imaginable. The victim died naked, in bloody sweat, helpless to control body excretions or brush away the flies. Thus exposed to the jeering crowd, the criminal died a spectacle of disgrace. By Roman law no citizen could be so dishonourably executed. The cross was reserved for foreigners and slaves.[12]

But Jesus turned it around. He used the shameful cross to expose the emptiness of the shame system.

We've seen that one reason shame affects us is that, this side of Eden, we find our identity in how others see us. But that's only because at some level we trust their judgments, and that gives them the right to define our identity. Jesus, who spent his life pointing people away from the judgment of others back to what God says about them, ultimately dealt with shame at the cross. In another of his articles, Neyrey walks us through the story of Jesus' arrest and crucifixion in John's Gospel.[13] He shows us how the cross questions the world's judgment about what is good and what is shameful.

At the last supper, Jesus knows he's going to be betrayed. In fact, Jesus himself tells Judas to do it. It looks like a betrayal, but actually Jesus is the one in control (John 13:27). Then, when Jesus is praying in the garden, soldiers come to arrest him. Jesus again takes charge of the situation. He gets up to greet them and asks them who they're looking for. When he reveals his identity to them, the soldiers fall down, humbled before him (John 18:1–6).

Next, he protects his own people, telling the soldiers to release the other disciples (John 18:8). As Neyrey puts it, 'weak people do not tell a cohort of Roman soldiers what to do.'[14] John explains that Jesus is doing this to fulfil the promise he made to God. Again, it might look like he's being arrested as a criminal, but in reality he's the one in control, and he's doing all the right things.

Simon Peter, on the other hand, is still thinking about Jesus' reputation. His leader is being arrested, so Peter takes a sword and attacks the high priest's slave. But Jesus stops Peter and heals the slave. In Jesus' rules for shame-free living, we are not to defend ourselves against attacks. The world expects us to stick up for ourselves, but in the kingdom, what's more honourable is being faithful to God's will and having the courage to suffer for him.

When Jesus is questioned by the Jewish leaders, they're essentially trying to shame him, but Jesus turns the tables on them. Once again, he refuses to play the victim, and calls out the elephant in the room: in John 18:20 he talks about how he has always worked in public, but they said nothing against him in public but plotted in secret.

The trial before Pilate is also about jostling for dominance. 'Are you the King of the Jews?' Pilate asks (John 18:33). But Jesus again deconstructs the game rather than playing along: 'Are you saying this on your own initiative, or have others told you about me?' He knows that Pilate is being manipulated, and he makes sure *Pilate* knows that he knows.

Pilate finds Jesus innocent, but that doesn't stop the shame trial playing out. The Jewish leaders aren't just trying to win a court case; they're also trying to win over public opinion, and again they do that by shaming him in public. Jesus is taken to be whipped and ridiculed, dressed by the soldiers in an ironic crown of thorns and a mock royal robe. But if shame is found in the gap between what you *are* doing and what you're *supposed* to be doing, then this is highly ironic: the world *should* be crowning Jesus and bowing before him, but they're only doing it sarcastically. They think they're putting him to shame, but they're really just revealing how shameful they are. Jesus' mock coronation really is his elevation to glory, even though the people involved don't understand it.

Even on the cross, Jesus defies the world's shame. He shows that he's an honourable son by providing for his mother (John 19:26–27). He's already told his disciples that he is in control over his own life and death (John 10:17–18), and now he chooses the moment of his own death (John 19:30). This means he is spared having his legs broken, so his body remains intact.

Finally, he is taken down from the cross. Criminals would be left to rot or tossed into a communal pit, but Jesus is given a proper funeral. His corpse is dressed and treated with spices, like the king that he really is (see 2 Chronicles 16:14), and he is placed in a new tomb owned by a wealthy community leader. What is meant for shame is, at every step, an expression of God's glory.

Who do you say that I am?

I've described the arrest and crucifixion of Jesus in some detail, because I think it holds up a mirror to the world. The early Christians had seen the Messiah come to earth, teach with authority and perform miracles. The world should have loved him! But it all went wrong. Jesus was arrested, put on trial and subjected to the most shameful death that the Romans could come up with. His followers were persecuted and kicked out of their homes. I'm not surprised if they thought, 'How did it come to this?' If the King had come, why did nobody else see it? How can Jesus be Lord of the universe if humankind put him on a cross? And isn't it shameful for us to be identifying with someone all the world considers to be a criminal?

Here is the first thing that John says to those early Christians: 'Don't trust people who play the shame game against you. They cheat. The world might judge you, but remember that the world took the best thing God gave to humanity and nailed it to a cross. Why should you listen to what the world says about you after that? The world doesn't have a clue.'

And that's why the early Christian community saw persecution and martyrdom as badges of honour. They had seen first-hand that the shame system is empty and hypocritical. If the world despised Jesus and his followers, well, that just proved that the world was totally out of line with God's values.

The negative evaluation outsiders form of and enforce on Christians is offset not only by considering the ignorance of these unbelievers, such that they are unable to form a reliable evaluation of worth, but also their dishonourable conduct, indeed, their utter shamelessness in the light of God's revelation of God's standards. To be shamed by the shameless is ultimately no shame at all.[15]

And this gave the first Christians the confidence to reject the judgments of the world and to refuse to give in to shame. On the cross, they saw that, 'having disarmed the powers and authorities, [Jesus] made a public spectacle of them' (Colossians 2:15). The cross put the world's order to shame, and brought into being a whole new order.

A way out

We've seen that Jesus refused to play by the world's rules, and this opens the pathway for the healing of those suffering from shame today. He offers grace, worth and dignity to people suffering from shame; he gives us God's rules for shame-free living; and he shows up the world's shaming judgments to be empty and self-serving. He's shown us that there's a way out.

Of course, we can't just apply this directly, like a kind of magic bullet against the symptoms of shame. We could try telling someone that they have no real reason to feel the shame they're feeling because the world has no basis to make judgments. But I don't think it would really help. Shame isn't a matter of logic; it's a deep-seated feeling of inadequacy and disgrace. You can't *reason* someone out of shame; people feel what they feel. For the shame-prone person, the voices telling us that we are broken and no good will always come across as louder and more believable than those that tell us that we are not seeing ourselves the way God does.

But the cross of Jesus shakes the foundations of the shame-based worldview. It niggles at our minds and sows seeds of doubt about the shame system. Maybe things aren't what they seem. Maybe the judgments I make about myself and the judgments that others make about me are not right after all. Maybe there's a game being played here – and maybe I don't have to play along.

And for those of us who have broken free from shame and can now minister to others, Jesus shows us how to lead others to freedom. When he interacts with people bound up in shame, he helps them to rediscover their God-centred identity. This is something that we, as a community of healing for shame, have to do too.

I believe that we can only break free from shame by breaking *into* a community of acceptance. It's hard enough for a person to stand out from the crowd and choose a radically different way to live. But if they're already feeling the weight of judgment on them, then it's nearly impossible. The isolation of shame causes them to withdraw further into themselves. How can someone who desperately wants to belong, to fit in with others and win their approval and acceptance, ever manage to break out of the shame system?

I believe that God can give us the courage to jump free from the cycle of shame and judgment, but I am also sure that the way that he does this is by giving us safe people to jump with, and a safe place to jump to.

Over to you

This time, I'd like you to read through a couple of Bible passages. This might be the first time you have thought about the characters in these stories from the perspective of shame, isolation and humiliation. Try to imagine how each of the characters was feeling, and how Jesus responded to those situations.

- John 8:1–11.
- Mark 5:21–43.

7

'I could have died of embarrassment'

Most sermons are too long, but once I preached a sermon that was too short.

In Japanese churches, like the one I was working in, people expect the preacher to speak for at least thirty minutes, preferably forty-five. Preaching the weekly sermon is seen as the pastor's main job; it's how they lead the church. Any less than half an hour, and the congregation start to wonder what you've been doing all week.

This was always a problem for me. I don't talk for long at the best of times, and it's even harder in a foreign language. Besides, I tend to think that a short, simple message has a better chance of being put into practice.

Anyway, one week, my senior pastor was away and I got up to preach. I knew it was going to be a short one. I got to the end of my notes and looked at the clock. Fifteen minutes. It was the middle of summer and I was sweating bullets. I tried my best to add in more Bible references, more examples, anything I could think of. But nothing else would come, and I found myself muttering a final prayer and sitting back down on the chairs at the front. Our church lunch would not be ready for another half hour.

The elder leading the service got up to the pulpit and politely thanked me for my sermon. Then he said, 'Are you sure you don't have anything else that you want to say to us?'

I didn't. What I wanted, really, was for the ground to swallow me up.

Wanting to disappear, wanting to vanish, wanting not to be there . . . these are all common reactions to shame. But why? And how do these reactions point us towards God's freedom from shame?

When shame attacks

Michael Lewis describes shame as a paralysing failure, 'a global attack on the self'.[1] Think about what happens when shame hits you. First, the emotion might be so strong that you can't make any reaction at all. When you finally unfreeze, your body starts to involuntarily curl up a little – the cringe – as you try to shrink away. I don't think we really believe that this is an effective way of hiding, but it shows that we are trying to hide away from the situation. Maybe it's also because our self-image is dented. I make myself smaller because my *self* feels smaller. We hide and cover ourselves to attempt to remove ourselves from the situation.

Beyond that, though, there's not actually very much we can *do* about shame. When we feel guilty, our feelings normally show us how to make the situation right again. If I feel guilty about stealing a bottle of milk, I can put it back or I can replace it, or I can own up to the theft and take my punishment.

Shame doesn't give us an easy way out. As we've seen, shame says that *we* are unacceptable. And if we're the problem, how can we be the solution? 'It is about self, not about action; thus, rather than resetting the machine toward action, it stops the machine. Any action becomes impossible since the machine itself is wrong.'[2]

So what do we actually do to stop ourselves from being ashamed?

Creating distance

I was at a lunch function at a friend's office and was introduced to Michael, a state government minister. Feeling pretty overawed and not quite thinking straight, I greeted him with a cheery, 'Hello Simon, I'm Michael.' He looked somewhat puzzled. When I realized what I had said, I became desperate to finish my lunch and get out of there as quickly as possible. Now I feel stupid whenever I go and visit my friend at work. Being in contact with the same people and the same place reactivates the memories of the shameful time. I feel the shame all over again.

Shame makes us hide. Partly that's a fight-or-flight reaction, but I believe it can also help to solve the problem. 'The goal of hiding . . . serves to prevent further exposure and, with that, further rejection, but it also atones for the exposure that has already occurred.'[3] Hiding is how we take the punishment of shame.

We can hide mentally, too, going to 'another place' in our mind. Shame has a way of dragging us down and constantly torturing us. Our minds play the shameful scenes again and again. How do we get out? I think we avoid the memories of shame by creating a kind of mental distance. We force ourselves to focus on something else, even if it takes a lot of mental energy to do so. Psychologist Thomas Scheff suggests that we sometimes try to distance ourselves from nagging shame feelings by 'a lengthy episode of excessive thought or speech':[4] we babble away at something else. I know that, when I feel ashamed about my behaviour, I often throw myself into my work, especially areas of work that I know I'm good at. It's my way of stopping being the person who failed, and rediscovering the person who is a success. I've also noticed that I have particular phrases that I say to myself in order to displace shame feelings: I tell myself to 'get out' or to 'keep moving'. I didn't realize until recently that this habit is related to the idea of creating distance.

We also distance ourselves in time. Michael Lewis wrote about a man who met a former girlfriend. She was still critical of his behaviour from the time they were together, but when they met up, he was able to take her criticism because he had detached himself from it. In fact, he was able to join in and agree, because 'it was as if we were talking about someone else'. He didn't feel any shame, even when they were talking about really shameful situations, because he felt that 'the past him was not really him'.[5] The person who was once ashamed no longer existed.

Finally, we distance ourselves through laughing. I spill a cup of coffee down the front of my trousers, and everyone is laughing at me. I also start laughing, at myself. 'What an idiot,' I might say. I don't really believe that I'm an idiot. What I'm doing is choosing to switch sides. Just like throwing myself into work, it's my way of stopping being the person who has done the stupid thing; instead, I join the ranks of the people who are laughing at that person. I separate my new self – the *real* me, laughing along with the others – from my old self, the clumsy person who spilled their coffee. It's another way of making the old self no longer exist.

Or I may wake up one morning, like James whom we met in chapter 3, remembering some stupid thing I've done, and say to myself, 'You're such an idiot.' Notice how I put my shameful self into the second person: 'I' am the person telling myself off, and I'm superior to the 'you' who did the shameful thing. I distance myself from the old me so that I can make a new me.

So our culture deals with shame by making the shamed person disappear and making a new, unashamed person appear. In a very symbolic sense, we are putting to death the person who was shamed. 'Shame's aim is disappearance. This may be, most simply, in the form of hiding; most radically, in the form of dissolution.'[6] When we are ashamed, we want to disappear; we want to cease to exist.

Honour killings

I believe this idea of dealing with shame by wanting to cease to exist is something that we feel in the depths of our soul. Somewhere deep down, we know that *death is the only thing that can cure our shame.*

In our culture, the death is only symbolic and metaphorical, so it's harder to see how death is the answer. We might *say* that we want the ground to swallow us up, but we'd be very surprised if it actually did. But if we look at other cultures, the link between shame and death becomes much more obvious – and much more real.

One particularly gruesome example happened some years ago in Iraq. On 16 March 2008, Rand Abdel-Qader was stabbed by her own father. Her brothers helped to kill her and throw her into a pit, while her uncles stood around to spit on her body. What she had done to deserve this terrible fate hardly registers from a Western perspective: she had been seen in public talking with a male British soldier.

Abdel-Qader's mother tried to stop her sons and spoke out against her husband's behaviour. She was beaten and had her arm broken, and fled into hiding. She said, 'They cannot accept me leaving him. When I first left, I went to a cousin's home, but every day they were delivering notes to my door saying I was a prostitute and deserved the same death as Rand.'[7] Two months later she was dead, gunned down on her way to meet a contact who was planning to smuggle her out of the country.

The Abdel-Qader case is perhaps something that we can't comprehend, but it's a typical example of the 5,000 so-called 'honour killings' that take place around the world every year: a female family member either does something or is suspected of doing something that damages the reputation of the family. It's often something connected with sexual purity; it could be extramarital sex, or it might be refusing the family's choice of marriage partner. Even being raped is seen as a violation not just of the woman but also of the honour of the family. Horrifically, this means that a victim of rape can then go on to be a victim of an honour killing.

The 'honour' in an honour killing is a particular type of honour, which anthropologists call *namus*. It relates to the integrity of the family's boundaries: men in particular are responsible for the boundaries of land and property and of the behaviour – particularly the sexual behaviour – of the women in the family.

If those rules are breached, or are perceived to have been breached, the men of that family are obliged to eliminate the woman who has brought shame to the family in order to restore family honour. Honour which inheres in the male members of the family can be seen as a parallel concept to shame which is experienced by women. Lost honour becomes a reality when it is made public, and can be restored by a collective response, typified by the collusion of family members in the death of a woman who is perceived by themselves and by the outside world to have brought shame on the family.[8]

Honour killings happen when the behaviour of the female members of a family brings feelings of dishonour shame upon the men. We can tell this from the brutal way the killings are carried out. There's a connection between shame and anger, and some psychologists talk about the shame-rage spiral.[9] Men, in particular, often deal with shame by an outburst of anger, but the anger can then cause further shame as we realize that we have lost control of ourselves. When Rand Abdel-Qader was killed, her head was stamped on, she was suffocated and stabbed multiple times, and then her body was thrown into a makeshift grave. Her uncles gathered around the pit to spit on her body. I believe this shows that they were deliberately using expressions of disgust and anger as a way to process their shame.

Abdel-Qader Ali was seen to have lost control of the women under his authority twice: first when his daughter 'demonstrated sexual availability' in ways that he did not approve of, and the second time when his wife challenged him in public. His family would remain in a state of shame until both the shameful bodies had been disposed of.

After his daughter's killing, he told a newspaper reporter, 'I don't have a daughter now, and I prefer to say that I never had one.'[10] Just like in the West, the way shame is dealt with is by annihilating the shameful person until they no longer exist. Ali imagined a family without his daughter; in his mind, he destroyed the old family and created a new family unit with intact boundaries and without shame.

This shows me that there's no other way out in our understanding: as long as a shameful person is not cut off and destroyed, the shame lingers. The only way we know of to deal with shame is to remove the shameful body through dissociation, death and annihilation.

But what if the cause of the shame isn't another member of your family, but your *own* behaviour? How do other cultures deal with shame then?

The way of the samurai

David Lewis, in *The Unseen Face of Japan*, tells a story of a family he knew in his neighbourhood:

The boy had been caught stealing and everyone knew this. It seems as if the father hit him, but he must have hit the boy too hard and somehow killed him. In any case, the parents then decided on a mass suicide. They took the dead boy and his sister to the family's hut in the mountains. Then they killed the sister and both parents hung themselves while embracing each other. When the children did not turn up at school, the school made investigations and contacted the police, who eventually found the family in the woods.

The boy's crime was public knowledge and brought shame upon the whole family. They could not face the public shame and gossip, so needed to escape it somehow. I don't know whether the father intended to kill his son or if it were just an accident, as some say, but it solved the problem of the family's shame.[11]

Suicide as a means for dealing with shame has a long and, in a sense, honourable history in Japan. Suicide in the samurai age was 'a process by which warriors could expiate their crimes, apologize for errors, escape from disgrace, redeem their friends, or prove their sincerity'.[12] Suicide in Japan is ritually unclean. It causes pollution. (Careful missionaries can save a lot of money by renting a house in which a suicide has taken place, as an agent will drop the price significantly.) But it's also seen as a way of taking responsibility for failure. Even today, it provides a way for a family or an individual to deal with their shame. Ruth Benedict wrote that, for a Japanese person, 'suicide, properly done, will . . . clear his name and reinstate his memory'.[13]

Just as in the West, the way to deal with shame is either death and dissolution or creating a distance. Japan is a culture where you're always aware of the community and how you're seen, so shame is more often external than internal on the shame matrix. Japanese communities deal with shame by cutting off the shameful member. They might stop talking to someone, or refuse to have anything to do with that person. It's not a physical death, but it's a *social* death.

The way Japanese people think about prison and justice reflects this too. We might see prison as rehabilitation or paying a debt to society, but in Japan it's a way to put the offender away and cut them off from society.

Another way we might deal with shame in the West is through confessing – what Brené Brown is referring to when

94

she talks about vulnerability. But in a culture like Japan, confession just doesn't work at all. It can actually make the shame worse:

> The voluntary exposure and admission of a fault (confession) and forgiveness of that fault become highly complicated. Forgiveness becomes problematic because to say 'I forgive' implies that I affirm the other person's badness, and thus forgiveness reaffirms his or her shame. Thus it is far easier to overlook, excuse, or forget than to confess and forgive. Indeed, *yurusu*, the Japanese word translated 'forgiveness', means to excuse, indulge or permit.
>
> . . . Where it becomes impossible to gloss over or hide the misdeeds the only recourse is exclusion, and in these cases there is virtually no possibility for reconciliation. And where the offender owns responsibility and excludes himself or herself in an act of atonement, there may be a certain moral resolution, but it is precisely the self-exclusion that justifies such resolution. Therefore it cannot lead to reaffirmation of the former relationship. Indeed, suicide, which is the ultimate act of self-exclusion, epitomizes the dilemma.[14]

Shame causes exclusion, and once relationships are broken by exclusion in Japan, there's no way to bring them back. A Japanese person will not exclude themselves from a situation for a short time, as we might in the West, and then come back into society once the shame feelings have gone; social death only works if you stay dead.

Honour doesn't help

So what have we learnt about how shame is dealt with? We've seen that one of the main ways that people get rid of their shame is through disassociating themselves from it. Somehow, they stop being the person they were and try to recreate themselves as someone new. In the West, we do it through hiding, running away, the passage of time or laughter; in some other cultures, the shameful body needs to be physically put to death.

There's a bit of a trend within the missionary world to say that God deals with our shame by giving us his honour. You might not have come across this idea, so please bear with me if not, because I think it's important to deal with as it seeps into what a lot of people are saying about salvation from shame. I believe at this point we already know why honour can't be the right solution for our shame. We said in chapter 5 that honour can't be a permanent answer, because it's basically just another fig leaf. It doesn't fix the main problem, which is that we're getting our identity from how people see us. We've also seen that a shame solution based on honour doesn't reflect the priorities of Jesus. Jesus didn't come to help us score points in the shame game; he wants us to follow him off the playing field.

We also know that shame in the real world is dealt with through disassociation and death, which leads me to believe that honour cannot be the answer. Why do I believe this? Well, try this on for size: a young Turkish girl is discovered having a sexual relationship with an unmarried man. The girl's father is ashamed by the loss of his family's *namus*. What can he do? Not much, but his friends, his colleagues and respected members of his village decide to help him out. They all gather around and hold a party in his honour. They publicly celebrate him, with loud speeches declaring what a wonderful father he is, how well he leads his family, how he's a wonderful member of his society and so on. Now he has been covered with respect by his peers, he goes back to his house with his family honour restored. Sounds reasonable?

Let's be honest: this doesn't happen. You don't honour someone who is not honourable. Only a fool does that, and a fool has no honour to give. The fact is that shame and honour are *not* the opposite ends of a spectrum. Shame is the bottomless pit. It is negative infinity. You can keep throwing honour at it, but shame doesn't go away.

The prodigal family

There's an example of this very situation in one of the most famous stories that Jesus told. In Luke 15:11–32, Jesus tells the parable of the prodigal son. Let's think about this story again based on what we know about how Middle Eastern families deal with shame.

We have a son who deliberately disgraces his father. The youngest son demands all the benefits of sonship with none of the responsibilities. By asking for his inheritance early, he's saying to his father, 'I wish you would hurry up and die so I can get at your money. But since you insist on sticking around, can I have the money anyway?'

He then goes away and spends all his money, and finally he ends up taking a job feeding pigs. It's hard for us to imagine how uncomfortable Jesus' audience would feel listening to this story. They would *feel* the son's shame. When I retell this parable, I have the younger son only able to find work cleaning public toilets. That conveys a part of how bad it was, but for a good Jewish person in first-century Israel, having to deal with pigs was even more disgusting than having to deal with human waste today.

Making it worse, the young man finds himself so hungry that he's thinking about eating the pigs' food. (I have him furtively eyeing up a leftover kebab from the bathroom rubbish bin.) At this point, he comes to his senses and comes up with a plan: his father! If he goes back home and makes a speech about how badly he's behaved, then he should be able to get something decent to eat again. Is he being driven by genuine repentance or just hunger? It's hard to tell. At any rate, he runs home, makes his speech – although it turns out that the bit about being made like a hired servant is too much even for *his* sense of dignity – and his father embraces him.

At this point, the father clothes him in a robe, symbolizing honour and status; he places a ring on his finger, symbolizing authority; and he places sandals on his feet, symbolizing freedom. A feast is given in his honour, and he is restored to his former status. His shame is covered by the outpouring of the father's honour.

Not so fast. The younger son is not the only character in this story. Let's think about how everybody else behaves.

On hearing of the younger brother's dishonouring of his father by wishing him dead already, the right thing for the older brother to do would be to beat the living daylights out of him and throw him out of the house. He doesn't do that. Then the job should fall to his father, as protector of the family's honour, but *he* doesn't do it either. Instead, the father agrees! By going along with this plan, the father is also responsible for his family's shame. He fails to exercise control over his family members and his hard-earned money. At this point, the family would be a laughing stock, friends would avoid them in the streets, and the father wouldn't want to be seen in public.

Next, when he hears that his son has squandered the family fortune and is now living like a Gentile, the right thing for the father to do is to say something similar to what Abdel-Qader Ali said: 'I only have one son now. It shall be as if I never fathered this second son.' Again, this isn't what we see.

Finally, the younger son crawls his way back into the neighbourhood. The older son fails once again to do his duty to restore the family's honour (and I think you know what I mean by that), but it gets worse. Now the father makes himself ridiculous. He runs (whoever heard of a respectable man running?) and he embraces his son first. He goes out and makes the first move towards his son, even before the prodigal has begged for forgiveness. Needless to say, this would be totally unheard of. Honourable men don't go first.

And so, if we're going to say that the father covers his son with honour, we need to ask the question, 'What honour?' The family doesn't have any honour left at this point, because their reputation is completely ruined.

The point is that *nobody* in this story is behaving well. Every single member of the family is covered in shame. 'Even at the moment of joyous celebration, the shame of the father is not removed.'[15]

So what appears to be a story about shame being overturned by honour is actually nothing like that at all. This isn't a story about honour being restored, but about *relationships* being restored *at the cost of honour*. It's a story about a father who is so desperate to be reconciled to his wayward children that he gives up all the usual rules of honour, status and prestige. He joins them in their place of shame so that, even if they are despised, at least they can be together. That is the sort of Father we have.

The gift of death

It's not too hard to see why we make this mistake about shame. We're used, in our Western Christianity, to treating all problems as if they are vertical problems: my sin is a problem between me and God. But we've seen that this isn't a biblical way to think about shame.

We know that shame is horizontal. Our shame is not first and foremost a problem that we have with God. It is a problem that we have with ourselves and our community. We've seen that some shame is internal on our shame matrix: we feel ashamed of stuff we have done when those things don't reflect our own ego ideal, the person we think we ought to be. Even if nobody sees me do it, when I trip over my shoelaces I still feel like a fool.

But much of our shame is external. We feel ashamed when we're negatively judged by the world, or when we think we're going to be negatively judged. We're ashamed when we fail in front of others.

And that's why there are two ways that people try to deal with shame: they either get rid of themselves – suicide – or they get rid of the others – honour killing.

So, in a sense, becoming a Christian is a *suicidal* thing to do. The Bible talks about becoming a Christian in terms of death and new life: you die to self; you put off the old self; you were crucified with Christ; the old is gone, the new has come; you have been reborn. The past you is not who you are now. The person who was once shameful no longer exists.

One of the biggest lies we believe about the Christian faith is that it's available as an optional extra to our comfortable, middle-class existence. You receive Jesus, you agree to a set of ideas about who he is and what he's done, you go to church and you're OK. Your life doesn't really need to change in any significant way, and if it does, the Holy Spirit will get around to dealing with you eventually. In an add-on, optional-extra Christianity, there's a continuity between who you were before you accepted the gospel and who you are afterwards.

This isn't the kind of Christianity we see in the Bible. The way Paul tells the story, Christ did not come to fix you up, to make you clean or to make you a better person. He came to put you to death. You have died. You are not your own person any more; you belong to him.

If I see the gospel in terms of guilt, where *I* am fine but *what I've done* is a problem, then being put to death is not a very appealing offer. I quite like being me; I just want my debts paid, thank you very much. But if my problem is shame, if the problem is that *I* am wrong, then dying to self sounds like something I really need right now. I don't *want* there to be continuity between who I was before I met Christ and who I am afterwards – I turned to Christ precisely because I wanted to get rid of that old stuff.

So the gospel is a way to declare bankruptcy against the debt of shame and to have the slate wiped clean: not just before God, but before our society as well. What Jesus offers us is the precious gift of death.

Baptized into his death . . .

How does this actually work? How does Jesus put us to death? Since the earliest days of the church, we've understood that the way we enter into new life with Jesus has been through baptism. You join the community of believers by passing through the waters of baptism and rising again to new life.

Baptism was a ceremony that Christians adopted from the Jewish practice of proselyte baptism; anyone wanting to come into Judaism as a Gentile had to be baptized, as a way of publicly showing confession and repentance. As we saw in the case of Japan, a public confession of sin is a humiliating thing to participate in. In her article about what baptism meant to early Christians, Maura Campbell suggests that when Jesus was baptized by John, he was deliberately subjecting himself to a ritual humiliation in order to identify with our experience of shame.[16]

Paul adds another layer of meaning to baptism when he writes to the churches. From this side of the resurrection, baptism was not just about purification, being washed clean from our sins. It also came to symbolize the hope of a new life: we go through death and come out the other side. In baptism, we re-enact Jesus' death in our own bodies. In Romans 6:3–5, Paul writes about how our death in baptism brings us into union with Christ:

> Or don't you know that all of us who were baptised into Christ Jesus were baptised into his death? We were therefore buried with him through baptism into death in order that, just as Christ was raised from the dead through the glory of the Father, we too may live a new life.

For if we have been united with him in a death like his, we will certainly also be united with him in a resurrection like his.

Between the second and fourth centuries, new converts to Christianity were baptized naked, because they felt that baptism was a public statement about freedom from shame. St Cyril of Jerusalem wrote about the reasons why, and explains the link between naked baptism, death and rebirth, and the removal of shame:

> As soon, therefore, as you enter in, you put off your garment; and this was an image of putting off the old man with his deeds. Having stripped yourselves, you were naked; in this also imitating Christ, who hung naked on the Cross, and by His nakedness spoiled principalities and powers, and openly triumphed over them on the tree . . . You were naked in the sight of all, and were not ashamed; for truly you bore the likeness of the first-formed Adam, who was naked in the garden and was not ashamed.[17]

So baptism isn't just something we do to join the church and get our sins washed away. Baptism *is* death and rebirth. How does this help those who are suffering from the burden of shame?

We know that the only way to be free from the stigma of shame is to die and to become someone else, to get a brand new life in a brand new identity. And we've found that this is exactly how Paul and the early church understood baptism – it's the way that we can begin again without shame.

Of course, there's a bit of a problem with all this. We die and are resurrected to a new identity which is anchored in our relationship with God. This is something that happens in the heavenly places. It's a real thing; what happens in the spiritual realm is more real than what is going on in the physical. Paul makes it very clear that the Christians in his churches need to think of themselves as new creations. So, in that sense, we *do* 'really' die.

But it doesn't look to anyone else like we've died. We get baptized one day, and then we have to get up the next morning in the same body, with the same people around us. Our life looks very much the same. Our shame *is* gone, but its reminders are everywhere. How does our new identity interact with the physical world?

To answer that, our solution for shame needs one more step.

Over to you

- Think about some embarrassing or shameful situations that you remember. How did you deal with the feelings of shame? What are your main defences against shame?
- Take a moment to think about what it really means to die with Christ: to your relationships, to your ego ideal, to your past. What else would you be glad to be rid of when Christ puts you to death?

8

The new life

One of the teachers at a local Christian school noticed a disturbing pattern. Students were receiving great Christian teaching, they were professing faith, and it looked like they were doing all right as Christians. But when they left the school, for some reason it didn't seem to stick. Many of them seemed to lose interest in God during university, and never came back to church afterwards. So the teacher asked one of the recent graduates to talk to her friends and find out what was going on.

What she discovered was surprising, and went like this: students graduate and go to university, and start living away from the constant gaze of parents. There they discover the big wide world of drink, sex and all the usual things. They still manage to cling to their Christian faith, even though they know they're involved in some pretty sinful stuff.

After spending some time sowing their wild oats, they realize that they want more from life, and they try to go back to the church again. But something stops them. They feel that they can't go back because they are *ashamed* of what they've done. Having left home as good Christian boys and girls, they're afraid of what people might think of them now. They feel ashamed of themselves. Worst of all, they find that the church makes their shame worse, not better.

This is a huge problem if we want to keep the next generation. How, for their sake, can we make the church a place of refuge for the shamed?

'I say this to your shame!'

It turns out this problem is nearly as old as the church itself. In fact, if you look carefully, you'll find that this was the problem that Paul was addressing in the strange passage of 1 Corinthians 6:1–8:

> If any of you has a dispute with another, do you dare to take it before the ungodly for judgment instead of before the Lord's people? Or do you not know that the Lord's people will judge the world? And if you are to judge the world, are you not competent to judge trivial cases? Do you not know that we will judge angels? How much more the things of this life! Therefore, if you have disputes about such matters, do you ask for a ruling from those whose way of life is scorned in the church? I say this to shame you. Is it possible that there is nobody among you wise enough to judge a dispute between believers? But instead, one brother goes to law against another – and this in front of unbelievers!
>
> The very fact that you have lawsuits among you means you have been completely defeated already. Why not rather be wronged? Why not rather be cheated? Instead, you yourselves cheat and do wrong, and you do this to your brothers and sisters.

Wow. This is a pretty intense passage. I don't think there's anywhere else in the Bible where we see Paul get so *angry*. In chapter 5, he's been dealing with sexual immorality in the church, and yes, he's uncompromising, but we don't get the sense that he's raising his voice. But when it comes to Christians

106

suing other Christians, something that hardly registers on our radar, Paul really lets rip.

He interrogates the Corinthians with eight rapid-fire questions; he is sarcastic and insulting ('Is there really nobody wise enough to judge a dispute?' Really?); he lets them know that he thinks they have been 'completely defeated' – not exactly a great way to build up the church. And in case they have somehow missed the point, he says in as many words: 'I say this to shame you.'

So it seems that Paul doesn't have a problem with the idea of using shame to bring Christians into line. But why does *this* particular issue get Paul so worked up? What's so bad about a lawsuit? I believe the two things are related: the reason why Christians taking other Christians to court is such a big deal for Paul is also the reason he chooses to use shame to correct them. Paul is aware that this community of Christians is still playing the shame game with each other. 'Well,' says Paul, 'if that's how you operate, two can play at that game.'

What's going on is that when the Corinthians took people to court, it wasn't just a way of obtaining justice; it was a way of bringing shame upon someone: 'to take another person to court is to shame them, and to do this before an outsider is very shameful.'[1] Bruce Malina says that lawsuits 'were used to dishonour someone or some group perceived to be of higher, more powerful status, and recourse to such procedures was an admission of inequality'.[2]

Let's take an example from today. Australians think of themselves as a pretty equal society. Everyone's pretty much on the same level; everyone's a mate. But if I have a problem with the minister of immigration, I can't get really get on the phone and say, 'Look, mate, this visa thing is really giving me a headache. You've got to sort it out.' The immigration minister and I just don't operate in the same arena. If I want a resolution to a problem I have with him, I have to go through official channels.

What the Corinthians are doing when they take another Christian to court is basically saying in front of everyone, 'Look at this guy! Who does he think he is? He's behaving like he's the minister or something, and the only way I can get sense into him is to take him to court.' A lawsuit says, 'This person is not one of us.'

The Corinthians were using the courtrooms as a way to show one another up and beat one another down. Paul talks about the lack of unity in the body in Corinth, and this is just another sign that everything has gone wrong. But this shaming behaviour is particularly unacceptable to Paul. His whole understanding of the church is as a community that doesn't treat people according to the world's standards. We're supposed to have checked out of the shame game. And so he is absolutely horrified to find that Christians are still trying to get one up on each other. For Paul, 'the Christian community in any given place is called to be modelling genuine human existence; if it isn't doing that, what's it there for?'[3]

Seeing Christians playing shame and status games against one another made Paul feel as though they didn't understand what the gospel was about at all. They had been 'completely defeated'.

So what?

Here's the problem: Jesus has turned the world's standards upside down. He has shown us that the things the world considers to be shameful are not shameful in God's sight. He has put the world to shame on the cross, and he has put us to death with him through baptism.

This all sounds great. But let's say I tell this story to my friend who's being bullied for having a foreign accent. I would quickly find that what we've got so far is only a partial solution. It doesn't pass the 'so what?' test. Jesus has put our shame to death – so what? What difference does it actually make to people like my friend? People around him still look down on him and tease him. It doesn't change his daily life. Jesus might think he's great, but he still goes about his daily life in a community that doesn't judge people the way Jesus does.

What he needs to really be free, to *feel* like his shame has been taken away, is a new community that *does* see the world the way God sees it. We need a community whose members are looking up and reflecting the image of God in each other, not looking across to what other people think of them. People can only live free from shame if they are in an environment that is itself free from jostling for status and position.

And that is why Paul is so outraged. The Corinthian Christians who are suing one another are bringing all that jostling back into the church. When they do that, they rob the church of its power to deal with the problem of shame. If there's jostling for status, power and position, new believers get drawn into the pecking order. If there's an atmosphere of competition and shaming, then confession becomes impossible, because it changes the way others see us. And that means, as our local teacher found, prodigals can no longer safely come back.

What would Paul say to your church? Have you been 'completely defeated' too?

Bringing the pieces together

We've found that church has a key part to play in the salvation of the shamed. The church is the place where new life happens.

We've already seen that the only way out of shame is to die; the great news is that this is what Christ offers to us. We're united with him in his death through baptism (Romans 6:3–5). What Paul calls the 'old self' in verse 6, the person we were before we met Christ, is now dead and buried. The person who used to be subject to judgment and shame has been destroyed.

Now if that were the end of the story, it wouldn't pass the 'so what' test. We also know that shame is a problem of where we find our identity. Shame is only a problem for me because of the opinions of the people I care about. We might not be able to change the opinions, but we *can* change the people. So baptism does two things: as well as putting the old self to death, it brings us into a new community – the community of the people of God.

This is why it is so important for Paul that the people of God actually behave differently from the world. The church is a group of people who have learnt to see others the way God sees them. People only experience freedom from shame when they see us living out this new perspective in our relationships with them. The moment we become concerned about our status and reputations and start judging people in human terms again, the whole thing falls apart. 'What orthodox Protestant tradition has not seemed to recognize is that the changed pattern of relationships is an essential part of the gospel of salvation itself.'[4]

The really clever thing about this is that it brings together some of the elements of Jesus' life and ministry that we've often kept apart. In our usual way of sharing the gospel, we say that

Jesus takes away our sin and we're forgiven, but then what? Ask a relatively new Christian why they have to go to church and you might not be given a coherent answer; and what's the point of loving our neighbour if God forgives us every time we don't? We know what to do with the cross, but how do we connect the cross, Jesus' teachings and the church? We can come up with answers to these questions, of course, but I can't shake the feeling that Jesus' teachings and the Jesus community are often tagged on to the end of a gospel of salvation for sin. We know they have to be there, but they don't quite fit neatly somehow.

But if the changed pattern of relationships is an essential part of the gospel of salvation, then these things – salvation, the church, the teachings of Jesus – aren't really separate at all. Perhaps 'this new group status *is* salvation itself'.[5]

What I mean is that, when I died and rose with Christ, when I was crucified and resurrected with him, Jesus gave me a new identity. I'm now a member of his body, the church. He placed me in the church because he knows that I need a community that doesn't play the shame game against me. And I'm only going to get *that* if the church is obedient to Christ's teaching. The cross, the community and the teaching all need to be in place if we're going to bring grace and freedom to others.

Now you are Christ's body

Perhaps that's why, in 1 Corinthians 12, a little while after dealing with the problem of lawsuits and Christians shaming one another, Paul paints a picture of how the church should be:

> But in fact God has placed the parts in the body, every one of them, just as he wanted them to be. If they were all one

part, where would the body be? As it is, there are many parts, but one body.

The eye cannot say to the hand, 'I don't need you!' And the head cannot say to the feet, 'I don't need you!' On the contrary, those parts of the body that seem to be weaker are indispensable, and the parts that we think are less honourable we treat with special honour. And the parts that are unpresentable are treated with special modesty, while our presentable parts need no special treatment. But God has put the body together, giving greater honour to the parts that lacked it, so that there should be no division in the body, but that its parts should have equal concern for each other. If one part suffers, every part suffers with it; if one part is honoured, every part rejoices with it.
(1 Corinthians 12:18–26)

There's a lot in this passage about shame, even though the word isn't mentioned explicitly. Paul uses the example of how we think about our own bodies.

I want to stop for a minute here and deal with something important.

I haven't said much about body image so far, but I know it's a source of shame feelings for a lot of people. We live in a world that consistently body-shames us with unrealistic expectations of how we are meant to look. And here's Paul seeming to talk about parts of our bodies being weak and unpresentable. What's going on?

Paul isn't a Gnostic or a Greek, separating out the body and the soul and thinking the body is bad and the soul is good. He's a good Jew, with an integrated Old Testament worldview that keeps body and soul together. And he knows what God said in Genesis 1 and 2. Paul knows full well that when God created our bodies, he made them good. In God's eyes, *no* parts of our body are weaker or less honourable than others.

Paul is actually making a distinction between how the world operates and how God operates. For the world, there are parts that *we think* are less honourable and parts that *we think* are unpresentable and so we cover them up. 'But God . . .' tells us a different story about our bodies from that which the world tells us. 'But God' placed every part in the body just as he wanted it to be. 'But God' sees there is no division in the body. 'But God' brought all of the parts of the body up to the same standard. Now all of your body comes up to his standard: 'very good' (Genesis 1:31).

You may want to take a moment to listen to God saying those words over your own physical body: 'it is very good.'

To be honest, just like Peter's vision of the unclean animals (Acts 10:9–16), the real point here isn't actually the physical body at all. The point Paul wants to get across is about *people*. He expects us to treat the people whom the world regards as outcast, weak, unpresentable and shameful with special honour, and to think of them as indispensable to the church. Theologian Dale Martin says:

This is not a compensatory move on Paul's part by means of which those of lower status are to be compensated for their low position by a benefaction of honour. Rather, his rhetoric pushes for an actual reversal of the normal, 'this worldly' attribution of honour and status. The lower is made higher, and the higher lower.[6]

In other words, we don't treat the weaker people in our churches better so that they can be nice, decent people like we are. We treat the 'shameful' people in our churches better because actually they *are* better than us. They're the honourable ones and we're the shameful ones. We give them special honour because the whole way in which we judge people is completely wrong, and Jesus turned all that upside down. Paul expects the church to determine status in ways that are completely different from the way the world does it. And it's not just Paul – James says the same too:

> Suppose a man comes into your meeting wearing a gold ring and fine clothes, and a poor man in filthy old clothes also comes in. If you show special attention to the man wearing fine clothes and say, 'Here's a good seat for you,' but say to the poor man, 'You stand there' or 'Sit on the floor by my feet,' have you not discriminated among your-selves and become judges with evil thoughts?
>
> Listen, my dear brothers and sisters: has not God chosen those who are poor in the eyes of the world to be rich in faith and to inherit the kingdom he promised those who love him?
> (James 2:2–5)

Once again, we can see that the apostles expected the church to be a place where the values of the world are turned upside down. The ones who are poor, those on whom the world looks down, are actually the rich ones.

My church recently held a memorial service for one of our congregation. She was one of those people who was a bit of a tough nut to crack. She graduated with flying colours from the school of hard knocks; she could be pretty difficult to deal with. Some church members had been reaching out to her and her family for years, but never really got much response. Others didn't quite know how to relate to someone so different from them. But towards the end of her life, she finally decided that she 'wanted what you's got' and put her trust in Jesus. She was totally changed.

As the microphone was passed around at her memorial and people shared their memories of her, one person after another talked about her 'simple faith like a child'. I have to admit that I really dislike that phrase, because of the way we use it. I think it's the sort of nice-sounding thing we say about someone who has not thought much about their faith, someone who's not become very nuanced and sophisticated in their walk with God – you know, the way *we* are. But this time I was reminded that a 'simple faith like a child' is exactly the kind of faith that Jesus looks for. She was the rich one and I was the poor one, and I did not realize it. She was honourable, and her faith put me to shame.

When shame comes back in

It's so easy for us to fall back into the pattern of this world, even within the church. It's only by the ongoing work of the Holy Spirit that we can resist the pull of our society and treat each other the way Jesus expects. After all, we've spent a lifetime in a culture that uses shame to judge and control others. The old self might be dead, but the body sometimes takes a long time to stop kicking. Even though we know that the church needs to work by a different set of rules, we still find ourselves jostling for power and position over others.

Patty Toland has written about shaming behaviour within the church in Latin America. In many of the evangelical churches of Venezuela, there's a really strong group focus: when you're in, you're really in. People are celebrated publicly for their contributions to the church. According to one person she interviewed:

> In the church where I am now they'll also give you a diploma when you've done good work. It's like taking note of what someone's doing. And this is what makes you feel honoured and worthy. It's a type of feedback showing that the work that you're doing has been worth the trouble.[7]

The problem is, when you're out, you're *really* out. Within some churches, there are different 'spiritual classes' of believer: upper leadership, lower leadership and then the rest of us – the 'ordinary believers'. There's an environment of envy and competition, and pastors and church members use the toolbox of shame to gain power and prestige over one another. Any church members who have been caught in sin are made to sit on certain benches at the back so that everyone knows, and they're not allowed to participate in the life of the church. Pastors will call out individuals' behaviour in their sermons. Younger leaders aren't encouraged and nurtured by senior pastors, because the pastors don't want the younger leaders to grow up to be more popular or powerful than they are.

There might not be anything wrong with honour, but when you bring the *desire* for honour back into the church, it becomes profoundly toxic. Jesus came not to redeem honour, but to put it to death. In the end, 'the pursuit of honour can lead to a need for repeated recognition and improved status through jockeying for higher positions, which often damages the church and quenches the work of the Holy Spirit'.[8]

And, of course, it's not just Venezuela; our own churches do the same thing, perhaps in less obvious ways. Christ is making us into a community that operates without shame and without judgment – but we're not there yet.

But now that we know how important *we* are for other people who are suffering from shame, it's absolutely vital that we get a grip on this. It is precisely because Christ upended, ridiculed and destroyed the world's standards that there can be no place within the community of Christ for bringing shame back in.

Restoring the shamed

While the church sometimes gets things really wrong when dealing with shame, there are other times when the church gets it really right.

Mark Baker and Joel Green, in their book *Recovering the Scandal of the Cross*, talk about how Japanese people deal with sin. They say that if someone messes up but their failure can be hidden, their friends will cover for them and protect them from any consequences. But as soon as the failure becomes public, the group will turn and protect themselves by isolating the shamed person. They give the example of a missionary caught in sexual misconduct. As long as the situation can be hidden, the person involved can confess and be forgiven. Eventually, after sufficient discipline and discernment from the church, they may even be restored to ministry. But if the affair were to become public knowledge, there would be no choice in the minds of church leaders. The missionary involved must leave the country.[9] Remember what we said about how shame is dealt with: the shameful body must be cut off. There is no other way.

When I was a relatively new missionary, I saw this situation play out in front of me, and I found it really frustrating. 'There is no other way' is pretty much the worst thing you can say to me. Surely we can make a way! Second chances are what Christianity is all about! I wondered, if these pastors weren't putting into practice the Christian principles of forgiveness, reconciliation and the opportunity of a new start following confession of sin, had they really understood the gospel? Weren't they just putting their own cultural values ahead of their Christian values?

But in the middle of this terrible situation, there was also a very hopeful and moving scene. At one point, as the Japanese pastors were discussing how they were going to react – of course, we knew what the outcome was going to be – the missionary knelt before the Japanese pastors, confessed his sin and begged forgiveness. At this point, one of the most senior pastors in the group simply knelt down alongside him and confessed that he too was a sinner, able to stand only by the grace of God. The message was clear: if you're ashamed of him, then you're ashamed of me. His action turned shame on its head. By accepting and identifying with shame, we can envelop it in a graceful embrace and deny it its power. The church living out the teachings of Christ can redeem the shamed.

Confess your sins to one another

Speaking of kneeling down and confessing, has it ever struck you that, in the epistle of James, we're encouraged to confess our sins *to one another* (5:16)? I have to admit that I didn't really take this in until I began to think about shame.

As a young Christian, I was always taught that we should confess our sins through prayer to God, and that God would forgive us. The only other passage in the New Testament that talks about confession of sins is 1 John 1:9, which says, 'If we confess our sins, he is faithful and just and will forgive us our sins and purify us from all unrighteousness.' In the Protestant church, we've tended to interpret that as confessing privately to God. Yes, 1 John says that God will forgive us, but it doesn't say anything about *how* the confession is supposed to be happen. I wonder if we've been reacting against the Catholic tradition of confession to a priest, and that's made us assume that confession is a private matter between each of us individually and God. But James is clear that confession should involve another person. Why is that?

A little while back, I received a long session of prayer ministry, offered by an organization called Victorious Ministry Through Christ. In their prayer ministry sessions, they encourage people to forgive those who have hurt us and to confess sins we have committed. With two counsellors, I read through a long list of categories of sin, waiting for the Holy Spirit to prompt me about things I needed to confess. At times I even surprised myself as God reminded me about unconfessed sins from the past.

The experience really transformed me, and it was another key step in my recovery from shame. Speaking out and repenting of those sins, some from decades ago but which I'd never dared tell another person, was powerful enough. But the real key was that, now, some people knew all those horrible things about me, but they still treated me as a brother in Christ.

I was part of a community that accepted me not for what I had done, but simply because of the image of God in me. That feeling did something in me that private and personal confession had never managed to do. I already knew that God had forgiven me for those things, but I also needed to be released from my shame. In the language of Christian ritual, I didn't just need confession; I needed absolution.

According to Michael Lewis, confession doesn't just give us freedom from stuff we have done in the past, but it also reduces the power that shame has over us in the future.[10] One of the reasons why shame is so powerful is that it's global; it tells me that *I* am the failure. Unless I change fundamentally who I am and how I operate, I know that I'm just as likely to end up in the same state of shame. Well, I know that the Holy Spirit *is* fundamentally changing who I am and how I operate. I'm not the same person that I used to be, thank God.

But confession also deals with the problem from the other end. I confess, I'm still accepted, and I realize that I'm not a write-off, after all. Confession helps me to remember that I'm not my sin, and I'm not my shame; I'm someone in whom God delights. If shame is the realization that I am not acceptable, then confession and absolution give me acceptance again. Despite the things I might have done, I'm still worthy of love because God made me.

And that makes me stronger against the next time shame comes knocking at my door. As Lewis puts it, 'that confession can act to reduce the anxiety of shame also must mean that it can act to prevent shame.'[11] Now that I know there are brothers and sisters in Christ who accept me even though they know the worst about me, I feel invincible. I don't need to do anything to *make* myself acceptable to others, because I know that I already am.

Handing over the cards

Confession is also the antidote to our identity curation. When I confess my sin, I'm admitting to someone else that I haven't got it all together, and that I'm not the polished, slick performer that I want to be. I'm inviting someone else to see the real me – actually, the worst version of me. If I'm still acceptable to them even at my worst, then I don't need to wear a fig leaf of respectability any more. The need to pretend to be something I'm not just disappears.

But confession goes way beyond that. Confession is a radical act of trust. It's not just that I lay down my fig leaves; I also hand over all my reputational playing cards to someone else. Instead of managing my own image, I'm giving someone else the ability to change how I'm seen in public.

What I mean is that, right now, there are members of my church who know things about me that, if they were to decide to make them public, would really mess up some of my most precious relationships. My natural instinct, the Adam instinct, would be to guard those secrets at all costs. But when I confess my sins to another person, I'm not just giving away all my deepest secrets to a fallible human; I'm also giving away the power to do untold damage to my reputation. The very fact that confession is possible is a way of telling ourselves that we've checked out of the shame game.

Perhaps this is why John Forrester says that confession requires a kind of 'ontological robustness'. What he means is that we need to have a strong sense of who we are before we can admit our weaknesses to another person, 'but the deeply shamed have only a shadow of a person to offer'.[12] So confession needs to be done gently and quietly. If we're helping people who are suffering from a particularly heavy burden of shame, we may need to find ways of doing confession together or as a community, rather than singling out individuals.

We're fortunate to have the discipline of confession available to us as a means to relieve and redeem shame. But do we really use it? As a child I attended a fairly high Anglican church which included confession and absolution as a core part of every church service. But recently I have found fewer and fewer churches where confession of sin is part of the practice of the church, either corporately or individually. Maybe we've bought into a theology that 'the only sin is forgiven sin'. Whether or not that's true for God, I'm pretty sure it's not true for *us*.

As the church drops the ball, the surrounding culture picks it up. Michael Lewis says that in the West we often see doctors, therapists and teachers as people we can confess to.[13] We also confess directly to people we have sinned against. We understand that the people we have wronged are able to set us free. But there are dangers with that: for one, they may not be able to forgive us. What then? Or they may feel that they ought to forgive us, which can place *them* in an uncomfortable and shameful position. They have to deal with their own hurt feelings because of what we've done to them, but at the same time they might feel they can't express that hurt to us because we're genuinely sorry and looking for forgiveness. Our confession forces them to swallow *their* shame.

There are many ways we can bring confession into the rhythm of our church life. Neil Cole, one of the pioneers of the

Organic Church movement, suggests meeting as single-sex accountability groups of three people, with a list of questions for confession as one element of accountability. My church in Australia runs a men's breakfast once a month, which has become a space for a similar kind of confession. We've heard many testimonies from people who have come through shameful sin, and that's created an atmosphere where others know that they can confess freely, with people who will understand and not judge.

That's something that is absolutely essential for confession to be part of a healing process: safety. We have seen that confession can actually make shame feelings worse, because it makes the person re-experience their faults. It confronts them with their own weaknesses, but it also exposes them to the risk of judgment, broken relationships and social exclusion.

The person who confesses must believe that they will be dealt with gracefully. We can only confess to those who have the emotional and spiritual maturity to take it. Suppose one of my church friends *did* spill the beans on my innermost secrets: my shame would be made a hundred times worse. Or suppose you confess your sins to me, and, after praying briefly for you, I seem to avoid you from then on. If your vulnerability is met with judgment, your shame will only be reinforced.

And so we find ourselves back at 1 Corinthians 6: our churches need to have completely checked out of the shame game. In *Grace for Shame*, John Forrester talks about the church as a 'healing community', and he gives ten values for a healthy church to encourage the healing of shame: 'genuine respect, warm hospitality, delightful diversity, attainable goals, good communication, healthy sexuality, fewer secrets, fun and games, small groups, and healthy good-byes'.[14]

Are we just saving ourselves?

I've said that the people of God have a part to play in creating a new community for the shamed. Our role, the reason Christ brought us together as a church, is to be a community that doesn't live by the world's rules. So am I suggesting that it's the church, rather than God, that saves us from shame?

Perhaps a way to answer that is to say that the church is the means that God uses to save us from shame. I don't think I'm saying anything controversial if I say that God chooses to use the church as part of his plan for salvation. I'm with the apostle Paul, in that Christian salvation is something that we, as a community, have to work out in fear and trembling. And God has always worked through relationships with his people. When Jesus ascended into heaven, he left eleven scared and weak disciples with the job of continuing to build his kingdom, and that's still the job we have been given. Sometimes God communicates his salvation directly through dreams and visions, but his fundamental plan is to work through us, his body.

I'm not suggesting that the church alone provides the *whole* solution for shame. Jesus is the one who has opened the way for us to live free from shame, and who has given us a new set of rules by which we are to treat one another. We've seen that it is only through Christ's death and resurrection that our old selves can be put to death and our shame can be disposed of. It's only by the power of the Holy Spirit that we can overcome our tendency to judge and rank one another; it's only through the power of the Holy Spirit that we can live by the values that Jesus established. Without a focus on the teachings of Jesus and the enabling of the Spirit, we would just end up back in the middle of the shame system again. We really can't do this on our own.

But he *has* knit us together as a body, he *has* given us his Spirit and he *has* given us the way we should live. He has given us all that we need to put shame to death.

Over to you

- Has your church checked out of the shame game, or do you still have structures and practices that support competition and status-seeking? How could things be different?
- If someone suffering from shame were to come to your community, what would their experience be like? Would they be treated as 'more honourable'?

9

Me, you and shame

There is no 'us and them' when it comes to shame ...
Shame is universal – no-one is exempt. If we can't talk
about shame and examine the impact it has in our own
lives, we certainly can't be helpful to others.[1]

Before we can lead another person towards God's freedom from shame, we've got to get our own houses in order.
If we're not going to be the blind leading the blind, we have
to confront the place of shame in our own lives, and deal
with it.

So what is the place of shame in your life? Maybe as you've
been reading this book you've already thought of some areas
where shame has been a key motivator of your behaviour. But
since shame is a subject that we've not had a great deal of
Christian input about, there may still be things that it drives
you to do which you're not really aware of.

When I realized how much my life was being driven by
shame, there were some changes that I needed to make: in the
way that I operated as a Christian leader, in the way that I
related to my family, and in the way that I went about my job
as a teacher. I hope that as we examine how I made these
changes, you can reflect on what changes you might need to
make in your own life.

Leading without shame

Identity curation is a particular temptation for those of us in any kind of leadership, whether within ministry or in our secular lives. Erving Goffman uses the metaphor of a stage for the way we relate to other people. We have a front stage, which is where we perform in public, and we have a back stage, which is where we go to be ourselves. The front stage is where the identity curation happens; the back stage is the place we hide things from the audience that would undermine our performance.[2]

We've already said that everyone is involved in identity curation to some degree. However, for leaders, the gap between the front stage and back stage is often much bigger, because other people want to believe in us and be inspired by us. We feel a pressure, whether from ourselves or from outside, to keep the front stage performance perfect and not to let anyone peep behind the curtain.

A few years ago, we came back from the mission field to visit our supporting churches. As part of that visit I had been booked to speak to a home group about our work. I had many good friends in that group, going back many years, and, while there were some newer faces, most of them had been wonderfully supportive friends to me and part of my discipleship journey. But earlier in the day, one of the church elders had told me that the church was not going to support us financially any more.

Now, here's a good question: is that home group my back stage, a safe group of friends where I can let people in to see what's really going in my heart, or is it the front stage, where I have to put on a polished missionary performance? Well, perhaps it would have been smart for me to ask myself that question before I arrived, but I didn't. I went into the meeting feeling crushed and let down, and during the meeting I let them in to what was happening and how I felt about it.

The next day, I received another difficult phone call from the elder. They had heard about the home group meeting and were not very happy with me. Why? Because missionaries aren't supposed to get depressed, of course. We're meant to be an example to the 'ordinary Christians' who are looking up to us, and that meant I was supposed to project faith, confidence and joy at all times. The problem was that I had shown my back stage when people were expecting a front-stage performance.

When our back-stage personalities are different from our front-stage performances, we're creating an ego ideal gap. We live a double life, curating a strong and confident identity in public, but keeping our weaknesses and doubts secret. It's the perfect recipe for shame. Leadership has been described as a kind of collusion: a follower wants to be following the perfect leader, and so they project their idealized image on to the leader. The leader, in turn, feels the weight of expectation on them, and plays the role that the followers expect.

We worry that if people see the hidden truths on our back stage, the spell will be broken. And so we feel that 'we must never under any circumstances reveal weakness or failure lest it undermine our status and respect and lest we lose our honour and the honour of the institution we lead. Consequently many Christian leaders develop a deep concern to appear strong, confident, and faultless.'[3]

I wonder what would it look like if those of us who have checked out of the shame system were to refuse to go along with this collusion any more; if we were to let ourselves be authentic and vulnerable (within appropriate limits) with those whom we lead. The crazy thing is that I believe my generation, and certainly the millennial generation following mine, would respect leaders *more* if they were authentic and vulnerable with those they lead, not less. Shame has trapped us into a Christian subculture that tells us we must fake strength and control if we want to be respected, and that's not even how the *world* works any more.

It's certainly not how Jesus worked. In his temptation in the wilderness in Luke 4, the devil tempted him to express his lordship through power, control and an impressive front-stage act. But Jesus refused. 'The source of Jesus' lordship is found in his relationship with the Father, not in the extent of his power and influence over his followers.'[4] That's where we have to get to.

As I've dealt with my shame and become more secure in what God thinks of me, it's made me much less uptight in my leadership. I'm not as worried about how I'm coming across to other people, and I don't feel the need to project an image of having everything together.

But I've also had to change the way I relate to others in leadership. I still catch myself trying to play status games with people, by talking about myself and my own achievements. I try to be more aware of the image people have of me, and I force myself to be honest rather than play to it: I don't pretend to understand things or nod along knowingly, out of fear that I'll look stupid if I say, 'I don't know.' It's become actually quite fun to say, 'I don't know', and I've found that I learn lots of interesting things when I do!

Shame and the family

At a conference on 'The Shame Factor', William Paul Young, the author of *The Shack*, explained how shame in his life held him back, particularly when relating to his family:

Let me tell you one of the most powerful things that shame does. Shame destroys your ability to distinguish between a value statement and an observation. For example, when I was first married to Kim, she would say things like 'Paul, don't mix the colored with the whites'. You know, talking about laundry, right? But I heard her say, 'I don't know why I married such a loser of a human being as you!' ... I was always on edge, needing to be perfect so that I can be one of those people that somebody could have affection for, approval for.[5]

I can relate to this. Despite my tendency to fight and show off in public, in my marriage I became a bit of a doormat! Why? Because, deep down, shame-prone people believe that if their true selves were to be exposed, their spouses would not love them any more. And so anything that I took to be the slightest hint of a criticism would feel like a threat to our relationship. This is why conflict is so scary, and why shame-prone people do anything to avoid it.

When conflict was unavoidable, I would move immediately to defending myself. If we're operating from a mindset that tells us we are not good enough, we use all kinds of defensive tactics to keep a relationship afloat despite the weight of shame. We feel the need to deflect blame away from ourselves for every criticism, real or imagined – or alternatively, we take the blame for every problem, whether it was our fault or not! We either blame our partners instead of accepting our share of responsibility when things go wrong, or we blame ourselves, hoping that this will make the problem go away. For some people, we might feel that we need to gain the upper hand by humiliating or disrespecting our partners; or, in extreme cases, we might become angry, vengeful or abusive. We give our partners the silent treatment, or fly off in a rage when things get difficult. We use all these mechanisms to avoid the hard emotional work that a relationship requires, because we're scared of exposing ourselves to shame and a perceived loss of status.

People who are insecure before marriage might think that getting married will give them a basis of acceptance and security which will enable them to love without fear. But it doesn't always work like that. It's just as likely that they will bring their own fears and insecurities into their marriages. Shame-prone people need to learn to see themselves as God sees them and to accept themselves as God accepts them before they'll have the security to relate to their partners without defence.

Because shame is such a powerful emotion, we can also find ourselves wielding it as a weapon, both consciously and unconsciously, towards our family members – especially our children. Generating a sense of shame is, unfortunately, the best way to get our children to do what we want them to do. It's an easy trap for any parent to fall into, but those who have developed a particular sensitivity to shame over the course of their lives will especially find themselves perpetuating a cycle of shame – doing what they know works on them in order to influence others, and so passing on shame to the next generation. In the immortal words of Philip Larkin, 'Man hands on misery to man; it deepens like a coastal shelf.'6

Once, after I gave a talk, a lady came up to me and mentioned that she had been suffering from the effects of shame for her whole life. She must have been in her sixties. I gently encouraged her to tell me more about it. To be honest, I was preparing myself to hear a terrible story of abuse or neglect that had scarred her for all that time. She told me that, one day, her father had scolded her in front of her sisters for putting the grill pan in the oven the wrong way. She had felt humiliated in front of them, and it had affected her relationship with her sisters and her father for all those years. It's easy to think that children don't know the difference between what is important and what isn't, but that means that, for children, *everything* is important.

One of the main ways we shame our children is in how we discipline them. Because he'd disciplined his daughter in front of others, this lady's father had put her into a situation of shame – it would have been very different if instead he had taken her aside to correct her calmly and privately. But to hear her tell what happened, it seemed as though her father had deliberately used the presence of her sisters to create a shaming experience. Shaming discipline is powerful, long-lasting and devastating.

More broadly, scolding and disciplining are ways that we train children with regard to our expectations of them. There are appropriate ways to do this, and there are inappropriate ways. Michael Lewis writes that there are four ways we can talk about why our children either succeed in our expectations or fail to live up to them. We can talk about the cause as either *internal* to the child or *external*, and we can talk about the failure *globally* or *specifically*. Internal and global explanations are more likely lead to shame.

If a child fails an exam, the parent might say, 'That was a really difficult test!' That would make the cause external to the child, and make the failure specific: it's about the test, not the person. Or the parent might say, 'You really didn't try hard at that' – an internal cause, but a specific failure.

Alternatively, of course, the parent could say, 'You're so stupid! You can't get anything right!' I imagine most of us would recognize why that would be wrong. But think about it the other way around. Your child learns to tie his or her shoelaces. Do you say, 'You're so clever', or do you say, 'You did a great job'? According to Lewis's research, it's likely you'd say the first one to your daughter and the second one to your son. Unconsciously, we train our daughters to make success or failure about who they *are,* and we train our sons to link it with what they have *done.* Our daughters learn, even through our praise, that they *are* their successes and failures.

This means I also need to be careful about how I talk about myself. The children of shame-prone parents tend to pick up on the language that we use about ourselves and apply the same values when they judge themselves. 'Simply being with a parent who is shame-prone is likely to lead to shame in children.'[7]

I pick up a bowl in the kitchen without realizing that it's full of water, and the water spills all over the floor. Without thinking, I say, 'Silly Daddy!' There's a huge difference between, 'I was silly' and 'That was a silly thing to do' – global versus specific again. When I say, 'Silly Daddy!', I'm teaching my children that my failure, small as it is, is linked to who I am as a human being; I'm teaching them that they should think less of themselves when something goes wrong.

The most common and powerful way that we shame our children is to show our disgust at their behaviour. We often do this through what Lewis calls 'the disgusted face': upper lip raised, nostrils flared, teeth bared. One reason why it is so powerful is that it is momentary and secretive; most parents don't even know that they're doing it. They might even deny that they're disgusted with their children. But children see it, and they understand it.

> A mother and her 3-year-old daughter were playing in the playroom. The child was asked by the mother not to play with the Playdough because it would mess her dress. The child persisted. The mother now raised the ante. She looked at the child, showed a disgusted/contemptuous face, and said 'Yuck! You're making yourself dirty.' The little girl looked at her, turned away, and then proceeded to pick up the Playdough and threw it angrily on the ground.
>
> This show of anger was a response to being shamed. In this case, the mother often used this shaming technique in dealing with her child.[8]

When we show our disgust to our children, it creates a sense of shame in them, and that shame makes them change the way they behave. It might be quite uncomfortable for us to think that our children disgust us, but Alice Miller has shown that disgust and contempt are common reactions for shame-prone parents who do not have a strong sense of their own identity.[9] Parents who have not faced up to their own emotional weaknesses will use this kind of contempt; it gives them a way to be strong against a weaker person who can't fight back. In fact, if we watch ourselves carefully, we might discover that we get disgusted far more often than we think – we've just learnt that it's unwise to show our disgust with people who are stronger than we are!

The disgusted face reminds us that we often shame our children without really being aware that we're doing it. Go to a supermarket or shopping centre and listen to parents trying to persuade their children to behave; it's a very humbling exercise. You may well hear people teasing their children, cutting them down with sarcasm, belittling their feelings ('Don't be such a baby!'), appealing to a 'normal' way of behaving – which implies that the child is abnormal – and so on. All of these are global, rather than specific, attacks. They focus on the child, not on the child's behaviour. It's humbling because it reminds us how often we do the same.

Finally, we shame our children through what Lewis calls 'love withdrawal'. When our children disappoint, disobey or disrespect us, we treat them differently. I know that when my children are behaving in ways that I don't like, my tendency is to want to disengage from them, to leave the room or to get involved in something else instead. I might even rationalize my behaviour by telling myself that I'm giving them a chance to calm down. But what I'm actually communicating to them is that my love and my presence are conditional on them behaving in a way that I approve of.

Love withdrawal leads directly to a global attribution of failure: it forces children to believe that it's not their actions that are the problem, but that *they themselves* are deficient and unlovable. Once again, we might find that we do this unconsciously, because we've learnt at some level that it's an effective way of disciplining a child. We may even have had this tactic used against us as children. But is it worth the cost?

As well as damaging our relationship with them and perpetuating the cycle of shameproneness, I believe that shaming our children gives them an inaccurate picture of the fatherhood of God. When we sin, do we think God is disappointed or disgusted with us? Do we think he can't love us any more because of our actions, or do we believe that he withdraws from us? If we do, then we've probably inherited an image of God from the way our parents treated us.

The God we see in the Bible is totally the opposite. Jesus' parables paint a picture of a God who is continually seeking out sinners until he finds them; who, instead of withdrawing, draws closer to us when we need him the most. But this understanding of parenthood is often so far outside our own experience that we find it hard to believe. If our children are going to understand that a loving God is not ashamed of them, the best way for them to learn is to see that a loving parent is not ashamed of them.

So how do we raise our children to be resilient against shame, particularly in the way we relate to them? Now that I'm aware of the way I tend to use love withdrawal against my children, I've tried to stay more present and engaged with them even when they are being 'difficult'. At the same time, I'm learning to be more aware of my own feelings – anger, disappointment, frustration – and I've realized that I need to deal with these in myself first before I try dealing with my child. I try to think about whether I'm using global or specific attributions when I speak to my children, and when they hear me speak about myself.

Finally, I seek to show them my own freedom from shame; I don't hide my mistakes or failures from them. I try to apologize quickly when I have failed them, and I try not to curate the image of being a better father than I am. They know I'm not perfect – they experience it, after all! – but I hope that they're learning that I do not need to pretend to be perfect, and neither do they.

Teaching without shame

After we left Japan, I spent three years teaching at a missionary training centre. I really enjoy teaching, but as I've explored the impact of shame, my attitude towards teaching has changed dramatically.

Shame can affect the way we teach in a couple of different ways. For starters, the classroom comes with an in-built power imbalance. The teacher holds all the cards. It's the teacher who tells the students what to do and determines how the lesson is going to go. This power, like all power, can be addictive.

> It can help our fragile egos to perform the role of expert scholar rather than elder brother or sister guiding emerging leaders in their pilgrimages . . . When my self-esteem as a teacher is at stake, I will seek to find my worth from my status in relationship with the students.[10]

I've seen this happen in my own experience as a teacher. I came to derive my identity from how I looked in front of the class. I loved to be the one up front, showing off my knowledge and enjoying the process of presenting. I might have been teaching the *subject*, but I certainly wasn't teaching the *students*.

As I began to understand the role of shame in my life, God challenged me to love my students as much as I loved teaching them. That meant changing the way I taught and how I related to the class. I moved from being the 'sage on the stage to the guide on the side'. I came to see my job no longer as being about 'me teaching', but as being about designing an environment where the students could learn. How could I challenge them and empower them to discover their own answers, to integrate them in the classroom and then apply them to their own lives? Arranging my teaching so that the class was more about the students and less about me worked against my natural tendency to seek prestige in my own activity – but it actually led to a much better learning experience.

At the same time, a shame-prone teacher is dangerous for the students. Insecure teachers will consciously and unconsciously use their knowledge to cut people down, not to build them up. One way we do this is by embarrassing students – maybe not intentionally – perhaps by singling out individuals and putting them on the spot. We can ask questions that are not genuine questions, but where 'learners expend their creative energies on trying to discover the specific answer buried in the folds of the teacher's brain';[11] or we confuse them with overly specific or impossibly open questions that they are not equipped to answer. It takes a while to realize that if the students can't answer a question the teacher poses, it's the teacher, not the students, who has failed.

Perry Shaw writes that 'teachers with high self-esteem feel at ease sharing something of their genuine self (within appropriate boundaries), and are comfortable with the shortcomings of others, graciously correcting error in others and honestly acknowledging error in self'. When I'm not trying to curate my identity in front of my students, and when genuinely I have nothing to prove, I can allow my own failures to be part of the learning process.

The first year I taught church planting, I was very insecure. The methods and principles I taught were really more a way of justifying some of the things we had done in Japan, as much to myself as to my students. Now, because I don't feel ashamed by some of the things we got wrong, I can invite my students to analyse the mistakes we made as well as some of the things we got right. It creates trust, makes the topic more approachable and more human, and it encourages students to be open with me in return.

And, of course, it's not just teaching. Our own self-esteem and our relationship with God and with ourselves affect the way we correct other people's failures and provide feedback in many areas of life. As we saw from the senior pastors in Venezuela, we can only genuinely build other people up if we're happy that one day they might do better than we're doing. But if we're insecure in our own position, we'll naturally try to keep them below us, and we'll use feedback and criticism to do that.

I believe those of us who are involved in teaching or standing up in front of others in some capacity – whether in our churches, in our workplaces or elsewhere – need to step back and think about what we're getting out of it. Does our position as a teacher of others boost our image, increase our status or feed our ego? Are we aware of the tricks that we use to make ourselves look good and to curate our identity from the podium, lectern or pulpit? Are we comfortable enough with ourselves that we can admit our weaknesses, ignorance and errors in front of those we teach? Do our interactions with them demonstrate patience and grace?

Even those of us who are not involved in front-line teaching will be placed in situations where we're responsible for guiding or correcting others. We all need an identity securely rooted in the image of God, free from the need to impress others or to seek our own glory, before we can begin to develop the image of God in others.

Over to you

You've read about what I had to do once I realized how much shame was a driver in my life. Now I'd like you to think what *you* might need to do. Please don't skip over this section; give it some time, pray and listen to God. Bring the topic before him and hear what he is saying to you. Here are some questions to help you reflect:

- What has particularly stood out to you in this book so far?
- What is God saying to you about shame through what you have read?
- In what ways do you shame others?
- What is your attitude to the judgment of others? Are you chasing approval, or do you feel crushed by others' attitudes towards you? Do you see the image of God in yourself?

If there are shameful things in your past or present life, it would be good to find someone that you can confess them to and pray with. I know this is hard. There have been things in my own life that I was sure that there was nobody I could tell, but I have consistently found that the power of shame is broken when what is done in the dark is brought into the light. You will always be able to find someone who will listen to you without judging you. God has given us a community in which shame can be healed.

Perhaps you have noticed patterns of behaviour where you either deliberately or inadvertently shame others. Bring these patterns before God and he will show you what's going on behind them. Once we begin to 'name the shame' and become aware of how shame drives us, we can then invite God to work in those areas of our lives and to prepare us to work freedom into the lives of others.

10

Ministering to the shamed

My friend Matt made a mistake. It was just a momentary mistake, but it attracted the attention of the police, and that attracted the attention of some journalists, and *that* attracted the attention of the baying horde of howler monkeys called the internet.

Because of his mistake, Matt lost his job. He's tried applying for other jobs since then, but the first thing many employers will do when they receive a job application is try to find out some more about the applicant. And if you type Matt's full name into Google, the first few pages of hits bring up some comments and posts that would make an employer think twice.

To be honest, I thank God every time I remember that I went to university before the days of social media, because Matt's story could so easily have been mine. Now we're in a world where there's a permanent, public record of all our shameful failures. Nothing is ever forgotten.

But imagine if it could be.

Pressing the reset button

Now that we have an understanding of shame, does it give us a way to explain the gospel to someone like Matt? I don't think it gives us a formula that we can use for everyone, because I don't think there's only one gospel message. Jesus told Simon and Andrew to follow him, Nicodemus to be born again, the rich man to give away his possessions, and Saul to stop persecuting him! While the presentation of the gospel has to be personal and relational, what we have learnt so far about shame can give us a framework we can have in our minds as we share our hope with others.

The first element of this framework is that Jesus can hand you a reset button for your life. Imagine if you could wipe out everything that Google knows about you, and everything that Facebook, Instagram, Twitter and YouTube know about you, along with all your search activity and all your browser history – yes, even *those* sites. You would be able to start again. The Bible says that 'if anyone is in Christ, the new creation has come: the old has gone, the new is here!' (2 Corinthians 5:17).

Jesus blows up our experience of shame because he blew up shame itself. He exposed its emptiness, because what humanity saw as a shameful death on the cross was actually the most glorious thing the world has ever experienced. He 'scorned its shame' (see Hebrews 12:2) and made a public spectacle of its power. When he dealt with people, he showed how the shame system tries to control them. In his teaching and throughout his earthly life, he showed us a way of living free from the expectations of others. Jesus shows us that a life without shame is possible.

The second element is dying and being raised to life. The Bible talks about the reset button through the language of 'dying with Christ' (see Romans 6:8; Colossians 2:20). One of my co-workers at the mission training centre realized that because she had died with Christ, she could no longer be offended by others. Everything people would say about her, they would be saying about the person who had died.

The fact is, I can't wipe out everything that Google knows about my friend Matt. If someone were to search for him, they might still be able to uncover those old inconvenient truths. But those things can't hurt Matt any more because he knows that the person they describe is dead. That old Matt is no more. The connection is broken.

Not only that, but we don't just die to all that the world thinks of us; we are also given a new identity based on what God thinks of us. We can live a life free from shame just like Christ did, because, like him, we're tuned into the voice that says we are made in the image of God. And through his Spirit we can access his life-giving power to hear what God says about us. 'I have been crucified with Christ and I no longer live, but Christ lives in me' (Galatians 2:20).

Third, Jesus places us into a new community and a new family. This new family is made up of people who are free from judging others and being judged by them, so they don't relate to one another in the way that the world does. The church is full of people who have also been through death and new life. They've all received this same new identity. Instead of looking to a faithless world to tell us who we are, we can know that we are free from shame, because we belong to a family that sees the image of God and the Spirit of God in every member. In this family, we continue to point one another towards the God who loves and accepts us. 'So from now on we regard no one from a worldly point of view. Though we once regarded Christ in this way, we do so no longer' (2 Corinthians 5:16).

The final element is that being in Christ gives us a way out of the battle for prestige. We *know* that curating our identity, trying to get one up on others and continually trying to present ourselves as ever stronger, happier, smarter and more satisfied is like chasing the wind. We know it's a battle that we can't win, because, even if the identity we choose *can* keep up with those around us, deep inside we know that it's not really who we are.

If you're fighting this battle, you're already losing. But at the same time, perhaps you don't seem to be able to quit. There's something stopping you from being authentically yourself, and it's that you only see yourself in the mirrored sunglasses of your friends. We all do. But we aren't meant to live like that. God made us to be secure in him, to be loved by him, to be in relationship with him, and 'if God is for us, who can be against us?' (Romans 8:31).

Let's summarize the gospel for the shamed:

- Jesus showed the shame system of the world to be a lie, and he showed us how to live outside it.
- Coming to Jesus gives us a new start, a reset button for life.
- The way out of shame is to die with Christ and receive a new identity. Now all of that shame relates to the person you were, not the person you are now.
- When you are raised to life again with him, he puts you in a new family that is not ashamed of you, and which won't judge you the way the world does.
- Now you don't need to live according to what others think, because you can hear what God says about you.

You might have noticed that I haven't explicitly mentioned the word 'sin' in the presentation I have outlined above. In one sense, this is totally appropriate. People who are burdened by the shame of abuse, judgment, misunderstanding, ostracism or bullying are more likely to find God through a confrontation with the sins done to them than through a confrontation with the sins they have inflicted on others. I don't mean to minimize their own sin, but, as we saw with the example of Job in chapter 4, we don't need to turn a shame experience into a guilt experience for God to speak. And when he does speak, we can trust him to put his finger on those areas of someone's life that need to change. The message *we* bring must be good news for the shamed.

In another sense, though, sin is everywhere in this gospel outline. Don Barns, a former principal of the college where I taught, describes sin as 'anything we do apart from God'. This is how we see sin explained in the first chapters of Genesis, where humanity's shame story begins. Adam and Eve sin when they seek knowledge and wisdom apart from God; Cain sins because 'in his heart he is not totally dependent on God';[1] the people of Babel sin because they try to seek a name for themselves apart from God – something we have all been doing ever since.

The Bible does not need to name these examples explicitly as sin for us to be clear that they are wrong.[2] Shame is generated when we look to others rather than to God for who we are and when we seek to make a name for ourselves without reference to God. Our experience of shame itself *demonstrates* that we're sinners, that we've lost our ultimate reference point.

When we share the gospel with those around us, we can point to the broken relationships with God, with our peers and with ourselves as evidence for our fallen state. As we disciple those who have accepted the gospel, we can put a name to this state and help them to turn away from it.

And when they do turn away from their sin, what next?

A funeral for shame

We've already mentioned, in chapter 8, how baptism is part of the process of freedom from shame in the life of the new Christian. Baptism has a dual meaning for the shamed person. The usual understanding of baptism – washing away the past sins and declaring someone clean and pure again – is particularly meaningful for the person dealing with shame. For those whose shame comes from a sense of being dirty or unacceptable, we can emphasize this aspect of baptism. Verses such as 1 Corinthians 6:11, Ephesians 5:26 and Hebrews 10:22 speak about Jesus washing us clean from our sins and restoring us to a state of purity and holiness.

But we've also seen that there's a deeper meaning to baptism. When a person is baptized, the old self dies and a new self is created through union with Christ. Baptism doesn't just put to death what we've *done*; it also puts to death the person we *are*, and allows us to be born again as a new creation in a new community. Baptism is a funeral for shame. I've found it meaningful to talk about this second meaning of baptism with those who are carrying around dishonour and disgrace shame. Baptism is both a new start at life and the start of a *new life*; when we celebrate baptism we can make it as meaningful a life event as a birth, a marriage or a funeral.

Baptism also creates new family ties. In cultures where becoming a Christian is costly and sacrificial, often resulting in broken relationships with family and friends, it's especially important that converts know that they're being welcomed into a new community. New believers, especially those who have lost their family in the process, need us to be brothers and sisters to them. Some churches do use the language of 'brother' and 'sister', as the early church did, but we need to ensure that we live it.

When a South Asian lady I know became a Christian and was thrown out of her home, she realized that the church's language didn't always match reality: 'Be careful when you talk about family and community, because I'm going to hold you to it when you call me "sister".' If we're family, we've got to act like it: being hospitable, being there for each other and literally welcoming people into our homes as a member of the family. When we really treat as family those for whom becoming a Christian has come at great cost, with our actions and not just our words, it helps to heal the shame of having disgraced their natural family.

There may be people in our churches who have been Christians for a long time but still require healing from shame. This might be because their sins or life circumstances have never really been dealt with, or it may be because of a new realization of the place of shame in their life. As we mentioned in chapter 8, we need first to reclaim the discipline of confession and to teach about the power of confession to banish shame and pretence.

There are many forms of confession – public or private, spoken or silent, individual or corporate. I believe we need to include confession of both sins we've committed and sins committed against us. The Bible speaks, as we have mentioned, of confession to God (Psalm 32:5) and to one another (James 5:16). Confession gives us a place to name the shame and to receive healing and acceptance. Of course, the acceptance is ultimately from God, but he makes this acceptance more tangible through those he has placed around us. He has given us these communities as channels through which his grace can flow.

Is your church cultivating the discipline of confession and allowing it to happen well? We can create time for silent and personal confession during meetings to allow people to bring their past before God. Confession can easily turn into a pity party for the shamed ('See what sort of person I am?') unless we follow it with expressions of absolution and acceptance.

As well as our corporate times together, there's a value in encouraging smaller, single-sex groups to meet regularly for personal accountability and confession, so that shameful sins and experiences can be processed in an atmosphere of trust. Leaders need to be trained both in the theology of shame and its salvation and in the need for gentle and loving acceptance and confidentiality when dealing with the confession of shame.

The ministry of showing up

There'll be some people in our churches who are suffering from shame but are not yet at the point of being able to unburden themselves. People who are paralysed by shame are constantly worried about how others see them and what people think. We can't expect them to find trust and acceptance for themselves; we have to make the first move, demonstrating that trust and acceptance to them.

John Forrester's book *Grace for Shame* explains more of what it means to be a church that deals out Christ's grace to those suffering from the experience of shame. He talks about the 'ministry of showing up'. When 'the shame-bound person loses hope of finding a way back into normal human relationships and community',[3] someone needs to knock down the doors and bring them back.

This is something that we see Jesus doing in the way he restored shamed people. In Luke 19 we have the story of Jesus and Zacchaeus. Zacchaeus was a rich man, which *should* have made him an honourable person in his society. But he wasn't – for three reasons: he was short; he was a traitor to his nation, because as a tax collector his job was to take Jewish people's money and give it to the Romans; and he was a cheat. He would have lived a life of dishonour shame. Everyone would have looked down on him.[4]

Zacchaeus must have heard a rumour about this man Jesus, who ate with tax collectors and sinners and gave them dignity and a new chance. The problem was, because he was a short man, there was no way he could get to Jesus. So he climbed a tree, just to get a glimpse. . . but Jesus got to him.

> When Jesus reached the spot, he looked up and said to him, 'Zacchaeus, come down immediately. I must stay at your house today.'
> (Luke 19:5)

'I *must*', said Jesus. There's an urgency in the way Jesus invited himself over for dinner. And Zacchaeus was overwhelmed. He couldn't have imagined that someone like Jesus would want to spend time with someone like him. And after being over-whelmed by the grace of Jesus, he responded with grace of his own – he paid back all those whom he had cheated, and he gave generously to the poor. It seems that, by forcing his way into Zacchaeus' dining room, Jesus found a way into his heart.

What does this mean for us? Just like Jesus' approach to Zacchaeus, we need to be ready to reach out to the shamed and to make sure they know we are on their side. This means we have to be the ones who take the first steps and rebuild the relationships that they need. We can guide them back into community. Jesus invited himself over to dinner, which is probably not a bad start. 'We cannot eat with a veil in front of our face. When the pastor joins in the laughter and talk around the kitchen table, shame melts away. If the pastor can come for lunch perhaps God has not abandoned us after all.'[5] And, of course, not just the pastor – we can all be ministers of grace for shame to one another.

Needing to be needed

Another example of how Jesus restored the shamed is one that has touched me very deeply, and one I come back to time and time again. It's probably my favourite story in the Bible. It's the story of how Jesus reinstates Peter, found in John 21. I believe this story also gives us some hints on how we can be part of bringing grace and freedom to the shamed.

After Jesus' death, the disciples seemed to have given up. Peter suggested they go out fishing again. Was he thinking about how he was going to provide for himself and his family? Was he trying to start a normal life again after the wild ride of three years with Jesus? Or was he just fed up and wanting to take his mind off things? Either way, the other disciples had nothing better to do, so they agreed to go with him.

And suddenly Jesus was there. The same old Jesus, performing miracles, always surprising them. The Jesus that Peter betrayed. I wonder how Peter was feeling. I'm sure he was excited to see Jesus. He shouted, 'It is the Lord!' and jumped into the water to swim back to meet him. But there's probably something else as well. I'm sure his mind was full of the painful memories of the night he betrayed Jesus. Before he jumped into the water, he stopped to put on some clothes. That wasn't a normal thing to do before going swimming. Peter obviously felt the need to cover up before meeting Jesus. He was experiencing an overwhelming hope, but also an overwhelming shame.

Let's remember that on the night Jesus was crucified, Peter had huddled around a charcoal fire in the high priest's courtyard. He denied three times that he knew anything about Jesus. Meanwhile, Jesus was being tried for his life. And then Peter didn't see Jesus again. Now Jesus was back.

Peter arrived on the shore to discover that Jesus had built a charcoal fire. I don't think that's just an incidental detail. Was Jesus deliberately reigniting the memories and pushing Peter deeper into a place of shame? I believe he was. But he was doing this so that Peter could be transformed and healed. *This* charcoal fire would not be the same as the previous one, and Peter would not be the same person as he had been.

From verse 20 of John 21, we can see that Jesus had led Peter a little way from the others in order to talk to him privately. With the new charcoal fire in the background, Jesus gave Peter a chance to undo his denials. This time, he had the opportunity to say three times that he really did love Jesus. And each time he did so, Jesus gave Peter a new role and a new commission: feed my lambs; take care of my sheep; feed my sheep.

Bishop Tom Wright gives the example of a man at a dinner party he hosted. The man offered to help with the washing up, but accidentally broke an expensive crystal jug. The man was astonished when he was invited back to another dinner party, and Wright once more asked him to help with the washing up.

The painful memory of shame was overcome by the chance to revisit the same scenario with different results. We can wipe out shame by accepting someone's failure and not letting that failure stop us from trusting them another time. 'I was useless' can be replaced by 'I can be useful again'.

This is what Jesus did with Peter. He gave Peter an opportunity to try out the same scene with a different script. Jesus healed the memory of the charcoal fire, replacing denial with love, and restoring Peter to a place of usefulness within the kingdom of God.

And that is what Jesus did with me. If you remember from chapter 1, a key part of my restoration to the church came as a result of being invited to participate in the children's ministry. It was not enough for me just to be *in* the church; I needed to *belong* to the church and to be useful to the church.

In a Christian community everything depends upon whether each individual is an indispensable link in a chain. Only when even the smallest link is securely inter-locked is the chain unbreakable. A community which allows unemployed members to exist within it will perish because of them. It will be well, therefore, if every member receives a definite task to perform for the community, that he may know in hours of doubt that he, too, is not useless and unusable.[6]

As we've reflected on Jesus' ministry to those suffering from shame, we have found that one thing he consistently did was to give the shamed person a way to become useful again. He had a need, and he invited the person in shame to fulfil it for him. Jesus needed the Samaritan woman at the well to give him water. He needed Zacchaeus to host him for dinner. He needed Peter to shepherd his flock.

Jesus recognized that an important part of being salvation to others was not just in what he provided for them, but in allowing *them* to provide for *him*. He allowed others to serve him. Communities that want to be able to restore the shamed need to make sure they don't come across as having it all together. If we're providing a complete service to the church consumer, we end up communicating that there's no room for new people to be useful. Perhaps there are ways that instead we can become creatively needy. Are we aware of areas where we're lacking and need a helping hand? Are we careful to allow and, if necessary, to create avenues of service for those who need more of a sense of inclusion?

At the same time, having an empty slot on a worship rota or giving a general call for help with the refreshments just isn't going to be enough. When shame has robbed someone's self-confidence and convinced them that they've got nothing to give, they're going to be unlikely to step up on their own initiative. Jesus' call to usefulness always included a personal, individual invitation; so should ours. Find a job for someone. Tell them you need some help and you think they'd be a good fit. Invite them to be useful again.

This might be more difficult for larger communities than for smaller ones; while the shamed may be able to find refuge and anonymity in a crowd, they won't find healing or purpose. But larger churches, too, can create spaces for smaller groups to connect, to form the relationships of confession and acceptance that we've talked about, and to enable those seeking a way out of shame to find a role for themselves.

Breaking the taboo

I gave a talk about shame at a men's gathering a few months ago, and a little while later the same group invited me back to speak again. What on earth was I going to talk about this time? I'd already told them about how shame works and how Jesus sets us free from it. I asked God what the next step for this group was, and I felt him telling me to make it personal. *Really* personal. He highlighted three areas of shame in my own life – social embarrassment, financial failure and sexual shame – that he wanted me to be open with them about. Gee, *thanks*, God.

But I went for it, and I was able to be open and honest with these men because of my own journey through shame and into freedom. Because *I* didn't cringe, neither did they, and so we were able to have a really good, honest discussion which led to deep confession and prayer ministry. If I hadn't been secure in the midst of my vulnerability, this would never have happened; we would have all been too embarrassed to have the conversation. Our authenticity as leaders sets the tone for others.

One reason why we must be free from shame as we disciple others is that shame itself is a shameful thing. We shy away from talking about shame and about shameful subjects because we know that they make us uncomfortable and they make others uncomfortable, and so shame stays hidden. And then it's difficult to teach or lead others in very personal areas such as sex, money and body image until we have broken the taboo around the topic of shame itself.

Our churches need to have an understanding of shame so that they can unmask the hidden dynamics that make discussion of these other topics so hard. Within our churches, we also need to hear the gospel for the shamed. Heather Davis Nelson suggests that our church leaders need to talk 'regularly and openly about their failures and struggles with shame'.[7]

In the Japanese churches where I used to work, there was an assumption that the leaders had to be models of the Christian life to others. This is a great idea in principle, of course, but the way it was expressed was that pastors and preachers would rarely, if ever, acknowledge in public any personal weakness, sin or struggle. For those in the congregation who *were* struggling or working through sin, the pastor might be an example to look up to, but they were never really an ally in the fight.

The Japanese leaders were still feeling the need to conform to the expectations on them, the image of being the perfect Christian and having it all together. While they were still bound up by these expectations, it was very hard for them to be ministers of grace to others. I'm sure that part of this was cultural – it's shameful for a leader in Japan to express weakness. But I believe this story also reminds us that, if we're still trying to find our identity and self-worth in other people's eyes, we can't admit our weaknesses and failures, and that means we can't create a safe environment for others to be vulnerable with us. Communities that are intentionally trying to bring freedom for the shamed will model vulnerability from the top down. Leaders will talk honestly about times we messed up, about our sins and struggles, and about our own journey with shame.

We can also use creative ways to break the taboos around shameful subjects. In some settings, this might be the only way to broach a particular topic; teaching and preaching might be too direct and too confronting.

What about stories? Most of the Bible's teaching is done through the medium of stories, and we relate to the stories of others. Recently I spoke to Birte Papenhausen, a German drama therapist. She has pioneered a way to disciple through drama that is sensitive to the needs of the shamed. In her 'Theater of the Decisions', a real-life difficulty is portrayed on the stage – let's say, a man begins to tempt a young Christian into a sexual relationship. At any point, a member of the audience can suggest a way to deal with the problem, but when they do, they are invited to change places with the actor playing the Christian and to see how their suggestion works out in practice. But then the other actors on the stage continue to develop the situation and apply more pressure on the Christian. Refusing to answer the phone to the tempter is one idea, but now the tempter comes knocking on the door. What now? So the audience member may discover that his or her suggestion is harder to implement in practice than in theory – saying, 'Oh, you just . . .' is much easier than having to actually get up there and do it. If at any point the audience member is not sure how to move forward, he or she can swap back with the original actor or invite another member of the audience to try a different idea.

This gives a way for church members to 'play' with their responses to difficult situations. They get to interact with Christian teaching on shameful topics in a way that's more realistic than through abstract teaching, but in an environment where 'everyone knows it's not real'. Even when people have been put on the spot and their suggestions fail, by acting they are 'becoming someone else', and so they don't carry the shame back to their seats.

After the performance, Birte and her team debrief the audience, thanking them for their proposals and seeing if collectively they have come to a sense of how best to handle the situation. The discussions they have produce a much deeper emotional connection to the topic than any sermon ever could.

The undefended church

Finally, I believe our churches need to be aware of whether they are curating an image of perfection *as a church*. Are our churches really free from the judgment of others? If we are, then we can be an example to those suffering from shame. But if we're still striving to impress people and maintain our reputation, the consequences can be horrific.

As I write, the Anglican church in Tasmania, just like many of the institutional churches around the world, is facing up to the scandal of child sexual abuse. Its behaviour in the past left a terrible legacy of shame, but the church has recently been impressively open and honest about what happened and how it failed. There will be huge sacrifices as the church is committed to providing financial redress to the victims.

The bishop set the example by selling off his palace. But to provide fair redress to all the victims, the church plans to sell off half its property, which will include many of its church buildings across the state. It's fair to say that this act of repentance towards the victims of abuse is going to require a massive change to the church's ministry. It's a controversial move, and some members are asking why this generation of believers should give up their churches to pay for the sins of the past. Bishop Richard Condie explained his decision in a pastoral letter:

The heart of the Christian message is that the innocent one, Jesus of Nazareth, took the punishment for the sins of the whole world. Sins that he did not commit. Making a costly sacrifice to right past wrongs is a profoundly Christian thing to do, and most worshipping Anglicans I have spoken to in the last weeks are prepared to do it gladly. The Anglican Church is connected to our ancestors who gathered weekly to worship God and built the church buildings we treasure. But we are also connected to those before us who did the wrong. As much as we appreciate the good parts of our heritage, we need to deal with the bad parts of our heritage too.

This is one of the best examples I have seen of a community 'owning' its shame. Before we can heal shame in others, we need to be able to confront and confess our own shameful history, together as well as individually. When a community reckons with its past, it models the principle that grace and repentance are more important than maintaining reputation, and that's exceptionally powerful. There's something attractive about a church that operates as if it has nothing to prove.

If we sweep our own sins under the carpet because we're worried about what the outside world is going to think, we risk coming across as a bit too squeaky clean, a bit holier-than-thou, and that makes it difficult for others to share their shame stories with us. Only a church that has suffered the pain of shame itself can be a place of healing to others, because it knows that 'there but for the grace of God go I'.

The problem is that lots of our churches are still on the brink of accepting their shame. The #MeToo movement has forced our institutions, including some major denominations, to deal with their own desire for self-protection, particularly in the area of sexual assault and abuse. A church that is institutionally insecure about its position before God will try to protect its reputation before the world by covering up shameful behaviour. Unfortunately, trying to protect a reputation at all costs may even mean silencing and discrediting victims, or downplaying the hurt that was caused to them.

Rachael Denhollander, a former gymnast who was one of the victims of abuse within the USA gymnastics team, has spoken in a troubling interview with *Christianity Today*[8] about how 'church is one of the least safe places to acknowledge abuse'. Partly it's because 'there is an abhorrent lack of knowledge for the damage and devastation that sexual assault brings'. When shame stops us from talking about important issues, it's no surprise that we're left ill equipped to deal with them.

But what really made me sad – and it's what really convinces me of the need to confront the defensiveness of our churches – was when Denhollander said that 'you have that dynamic with evangelical churches where you have the reputation on the line and the perceived reputation of the gospel of Christ'. Because she stood up for victims of sexual abuse within churches, she was seen to be dragging the church and the message of the church into disrepute before the non-Christian world.

We've seen all along that the root of shame-prone insecurity is a failure to reflect the image of God and to prefer the images that we create for ourselves. When churches fail to be transparent and authentic, when they prefer to live in the cover-up than to live in the truth, what they're really demonstrating is a lack of faith. They feel that the world would respect the Christian message more if it were expressed through a curated identity – a fake identity – rather than through its true identity. They believe that Jesus needs the church to handle his public relations. But, as Denhollander says, 'Jesus Christ does not need your protection; he needs your obedience.'

Does your church have a fake identity which it is curating? It might not be over something as dark as sexual abuse. But, in small ways too, we can prefer the image to the reality. Is your church trying to appear bigger than it really is, more influential than it really is, better than it really is, more holy than it really is? Does it oversell itself and its community with slick marketing to try to make a bigger impact on the world outside?

If a church is concerned with its own image, it cannot be a home for the shamed. After all, how can we offer freedom from the shame system if we're still trapped inside it? We're only going to see openness and authenticity *in* our churches when we model openness and authenticity *as* churches.

So let's be risky with our reputations, and radically authentic. We can leave God to look after *his* reputation; he's big enough to be able to handle it. Let's be aware every time we're tempted to inflate our numbers or oversell our religious products and services, and let's be ruthless in cutting off all attempts at image curation before they start. I'd rather be in a church that was gloriously mediocre than one that was desperately pretending not to be, and I believe many other people of my generation would say the same.

Over to you

We've looked at a number of ways that, as churches and as individuals within our churches, we can minister grace and freedom to those suffering from shame. As we come to the end of our journey of understanding shame, I'd like you to think about what you're going to do next.

- Do you now feel comfortable sharing the gospel in a way that makes sense for people suffering from shame? If not, have a look over the first section in this chapter again, and practise explaining to a friend.
- How are you going to make baptisms funerals for shame? Maybe you're not involved in baptizing others, but are there ways you can show new converts that they are family? How can you be part of giving them a new social identity?
- How is confession done in your community? Do you have people to whom you can openly confess your sins and your shame? Could you help to provide a safe space for others to unburden themselves?
- Are there people you know who are suffering from shame? Do you need to invite yourself over to spend time with them, or find some other way to break into their life? And is there a meaningful job that you can give them to do, to let them know that they are still useful and valued?
- Is shame itself a taboo in your church? Could you be part of breaking that down and helping others to see what shame is doing to them? Of course, it means that you would need to be vulnerable and brave before others. What needs to happen before you can do that?
- Is your church trying to impress? How can you contribute to making it more real?

Thank you

I want to finish by saying thank you for joining me on this journey through shame, especially if it's been a confronting one for you.

I really believe that shame is a key factor for us to understand our society better and to understand ourselves better. But because it's something that we don't talk much about in the Christian world, we've often lacked the tools to help people suffering from it. I hope that this book has brought you greater sensitivity to how shame affects you and the people around you. I also hope that you will be a channel through which God will heal the shame of others. He longs for his people to hear his voice, and to stand before him, unashamed.

Notes

Acknowledgments

1 Robert Wadsworth Lowry (1826–99), 'How Can I Keep from Singing', public domain.

Introduction: shame uncovered

1 Ian 'Watto' Watson, *Champion Blokes 'Shed' Their Shame!* (Woody Point, Queensland: Watto Books, 2015), p. 10.

1 Feeling ashamed of my guilt

1 Augustine, *Confessions*, 2:1 (trans. Henry Chadwick) (Oxford: Oxford University Press, 2008).

2 Augustine, *Confessions*, 2:4.

3 Augustine, *Confessions*, 2:8.

4 Augustine, *Confessions*, 2:16–19.

5 I'm exaggerating, but only a little bit. Geert Hofstede's research into cultural dimensions found that Australia came second in his 'individualism dimension' with a score of 90, just beaten by the USA at 91. Geert Hofstede, Gert Jan Hofstede and Michael Minkov, *Cultures and Organizations: Software of the Mind* (London: McGraw-Hill, 1991), p. 95.

6 Sarah Michael, '"OK people, take a look at this creep": Man who mum shamed on Facebook because she thought he was taking photos of her kids . . . was just taking a selfie in front of a Darth Vader display to show HIS children', *Daily Mail*, 8 May 2015, available at <https://www.dailymail.co.uk/news/article-3073095/

Mother-mistakenly-shames-dad-thought-taking-photos-kids-
Facebook-post-shared-hundreds-actually-taking-selfie-Star-
Wars-display-children.html>.

7 See, for example, Jack Holmes, 'The Death of Shame, or the Rise
of Shamelessness?', *Esquire*, 31 January 2018.

8 Donald Capps, *The Depleted Self: Sin in a Narcissistic Age*
(Minneapolis, MN: Fortress Press, 1993), p. 3.

9 Roland Muller, *Honor and Shame: Unlocking the Door*
(Philadelphia, PA: Xlibris, 2001), p. 52.

10 Augustine, *Confessions*, 10:2.

11 Augustine, *Confessions*, 10:30.

12 Augustine, *Confessions*, 10:30.

13 Heather Davis Nelson, *Unashamed: Healing Our Brokenness
and Finding Freedom from Shame* (Wheaton, IL: Crossway
Books, 2016), p. 102.

14 Heather Davis Nelson, *Unashamed*, p. 102.

2 In the beginning

1 Michael Lewis, *Shame: The Exposed Self* (New York, NY: Free
Press, 1995), p. 84.

2 Timothy Tennent, 'Anthropology: Human Identity in Shame-
Based Cultures of the Far East', in *Theology in the Context of
World Christianity: How the Global Church Is Influencing the
Way We Think about and Discuss Theology* (Grand Rapids, MI:
Zondervan, 2007), p. 101.

3 Tennent, 'Anthropology', p. 92.

4 Christopher Wright, *The God I Don't Understand: Reflections
on Tough Questions of Faith* (Grand Rapids, MI: Zondervan,
2008), chapter 7.

5 Gerhard von Rad, *Genesis: A Commentary* (London: SCM
Press, 1972), p. 91.

6 Claus Westermann, *Genesis 1–11: A Continental Commentary*, Volume 1 (trans. John J Scullion) (Minneapolis, Fortress, 1994), p. 253.

7 New English Translation.

8 Randal Buth, 'A Faith That Grows', in Milton Eng and Lee M. Fields (eds), *Devotions on the Hebrew Bible* (Grand Rapids, MI: Zondervan, 2015), p. 15.

9 See Dan Lé, *The Naked Christ: An Atonement Model for a Body-Obsessed Culture*, DDCT 7 (Eugene, OR: Wipf & Stock, 2012), p. 100. Also Frank Crüsemann, 'Was ist und wonach fragt die erste Frage der Bibel? Oder: das Thema Sham als "Schlüssel der Paradiesgeschiste"', in *Fragen Wider die Antworten: Festschrift für Jürgen Ebach zum 65. Geburtstag* (Gütersloh: Gütersloher Verlagshaud, 2010), pp. 63–79.

10 David W. Cotter, *Genesis*, Berit Olam: Studies in Hebrew Narrative and Poetry (Collegeville: MN, Liturgical Press, 2003), p. 34.

11 Bill T. Arnold, *Genesis*, NCBC (Cambridge: Cambridge University Press, 2009), p. 66.

12 Donald L. Nathanson (ed.), *The Many Faces of Shame* (New York and London: The Guilford Press, 1995), p. 8.

13 Henri Blocher, *In The Beginning: The Opening Chapters of Genesis* (Leicester: InterVarsity Press, 1984), p. 173.

14 Dietrich Bonhoeffer, *Ethics* (London: SCM Press, 1995), p. 145, emphasis mine.

15 C. Norman Kraus, *Jesus Christ Our Lord: Christology from a Disciple's Perspective* (Scottdale, PA: Herald Press, 1990), p. 212.

16 J. M. Sasson, 'we lō' yitbōšāšû (Gen 2,25) and its Implications', *Biblica*, 66 (1985): 418–21.

17 Henri Blocher, *In The Beginning*, p. 177.

18 Günter Harry Seidler, *In Others' Eyes: An Analysis of Shame.* (New York, NY: International Universities Press, 2000), p. 67.

19 Victor P. Hamilton, *The Book of Genesis: Chapters 1–17*, NICOT (Grand Rapids, MI: Eerdmans, 1990), p. 193.

20 Henri Blocher, *In The Beginning*, p. 173.

21 Henri Blocher, *In The Beginning*, p. 173.

22 Claus Westermann, *Genesis 1–11*, p. 236.

23 Claus Westermann, *Genesis*, Volume 1 (Edinburgh: T & T Clark, 1995), p. 269.

24 Dietrich Bonhoeffer, *Creation and Fall: A Theological Exposition of Genesis 1–3* (New York, NY: McMillan, 1959), p. 90.

25 Bonhoeffer, *Ethics*, pp. 147–8.

26 Bonhoeffer, *Ethics*, pp. 147–8.

27 Gerhard von Rad, *Genesis: A Commentary*, p. 91.

28 See Sam Chan, *Evangelism in a Skeptical World* (Grand Rapids, MI: Zondervan, 2018) pp. 77–8, and also Ed Stetzer, 'One-on-One with Sam Chan on Evangelism in a Skeptical World', *Christianity Today*, 24 April 2018, available at <https://www.christianitytoday.com/edstetzer/2018/april/one-on-one-with-sam-chan-on-evangelism-in-skeptical-world.html>.

3 What is shame?

1 Farah Farouque, 'Proud convict past an evolutionary lesson for snooty Darwin', *Sydney Morning Herald*, 26 January 2009.

2 Günter Harry Seidler, *In Others' Eyes: An Analysis of Shame* (New York, NY: International Universities Press, 2000), p. 121.

3 Marvin Minsky, *The Emotion Machine: Commonsense Thinking, Artificial Intelligence, and the Future of the Human Mind* (London: Simon and Schuster, 2006), p. 97.

4 Melissa V. Harris-Perry, *Sister Citizen: Shame, Stereotypes, and Black Women in America* (Yale University Press, 2013).

5 Günter Harry Seidler, *In Others' Eyes*, p. 232.

6 Merle A. Fossum and Marilyn J. Mason, *Facing Shame: Families in Recovery* (London: W. W. Norton, 1986), p. 5.

7 John Bradshaw, *Healing the Shame that Binds You* (Deerfield Beach, FL: Health Communications, 2006), p. 10.

8 Donald Capps, *The Depleted Self: Sin in a Narcissistic Age* (Minneapolis, MN: Fortress Press, 1993), p. 35.

9 Michael Lewis, *Shame: The Exposed Self* (New York, NY: Free Press, 1995), p. 63.

4 Telling guilt from shame

1 'Smith's Shame', *The Australian*, 26 March 2018.

2 'It makes no sense to say of one action that it is *more* prohibited or obligatory or ought than another action.' Julien A. Deonna, Raffaele Rodogno and Fabrice Teroni, *In Defense of Shame: The Faces of An Emotion* (New York, NY: Oxford University Press, 2012), p. 79.

3 Deonna, Rodogno and Teroni, *In Defense of Shame*, p. 80.

4 I got this idea from Robert H. Albers, *Shame: A Faith Perspective* (London: Psychology Press, 1995), which makes the link between Job and confusing guilt and shame.

5 Heather Davis Nelson, *Unashamed: Healing Our Brokenness and Finding Freedom from Shame* (Wheaton, IL: Crossway Books, 2016), p. 102.

6 Michael Lewis, *Shame: The Exposed Self* (New York, NY: Free Press, 1995), p. 76.

7 Donald Capps, *The Depleted Self: Sin in a Narcissistic Age* (Minneapolis, MN: Fortress Press, 1993), p. 75.

8 Léon Wurmser, *The Mask of Shame* (Northvale, NJ: Jason Aronson Inc, 1994), p. 51.

9 Wurmser, *The Mask of Shame*, p. 85.

10 Wurmser, *The Mask of Shame*, p. 51.

11 'Recode Decode with Kara Swisher' podcast, at Eric Johnson, 'Elites like Amazon's Jeff Bezos think they're being philanthropic. But they could do so much more.', *Vox*, 3 October 2018, available at <https://www.recode.net/2018/10/3/17930990/anand-giridharadas-winners-take-all-book-changing-world-kara-swisher-decode-podcast-jeff-bezos>.

12 James W. Fowler, *Faithful Change: The Personal and Public Challenges of Postmodern Life* (Nashville, TN: Abingdon, 1996), p. 92.

13 E. Randolph Richards and Brandon J. O'Brien, *Misreading Scripture with Western Eyes: Removing Cultural Blinders to Better Understand the Bible* (Downers Grove, IL: InterVarsity Press, 2012) contains an excellent treatment of the role of shame in the David and Bathsheba story.

14 But maybe not – see Richards and O'Brien, *Misreading Scripture with Western Eyes*, pp. 126–7, where the authors argue that David is still not really taking personal responsibility for his sin in Psalm 51.

5 You are not your Facebook profile

1 Makoto Natsume, *'Sumairu Kamen' Shoukougun: Honto no Egao no Torimodioshikata* (*'Smile Mask' Syndrome: How to Get Your Real Smile Back*), (Tokyo: NHK Publishing, 2006).

2 Ruth Ostrow, 'Mistaken Identity', *The Australian*, 18 May 2018, p. 18.

3 Sarah Marsh, 'The pressure of perfection: five women tell their stories', *The Guardian*, 14 October 2016, available at <https://www.theguardian.com/commentisfree/2016/oct/14/perfect-girls-five-women-stories-mental-health>.

4 Ana Marie Cox, 'Celebrities aren't the only ones who struggle to appear perfect — or who need help', *Washington Post*, 9 June 2018, available at <https://www.washingtonpost.com/news/posteverything/wp/2018/06/09/celebrities-arent-the-only-ones-who-struggle-to-appear-perfect-or-who-need-help/?utm_term=.f0471f7aca91>.

5 Heather Davis Nelson, *Unashamed: Healing Our Brokenness and Finding Freedom from Shame* (Wheaton, IL: Crossway Books, 2016), p. 73.

6 Roland Muller, *Honor and Shame: Unlocking the Door* (Philadelphia, PA: Xlibris, 2001).

7 Robert Albers, *Shame: A Faith Perspective* (London: Psychology Press, 1995), p. 96.

8 Stanley Grenz, 'Social God', in *Personal Identity in Theological Perspective* (edited by Richard Lints, Michael S. Horton and Mark R. Talbot) (Grand Rapids, MI: William B. Eerdmans, 2006), p. 77.

9 'The individual experiences himself as such, not directly, but only indirectly, from the particular standpoints of other individual members of the same social group, or from the generalized standpoint of the social group as a whole to which he belongs.' George Herbert Mead, *Mind, Self and Society* (Chicago: University of Chicago Press, 1934), p. 138.

10 Brené Brown, *The Gifts of Imperfection: Let Go of Who You Think You're Supposed to Be and Embrace Who You Are* (Center City, MN: Hazelden, 2010), p. 50.

11 Brené Brown, *The Gifts of Imperfection*, p. 42.

12 Paul Gilbert, *The Compassionate Mind* (Oakland, CA: New Harbinger Publications, 2010), p. 309.

13 Calvin, *Institutes*, 1,1,2.

14 Donald E. Gowan, *Genesis 1–11: From Eden to Babel* (Grand
 Rapids, MI: Eerdmans, 1988), p. 55.

15 Dietrich Bonhoeffer, *Ethics* (London: SCM Press,1955),
 p. 146.

16 Walter Brueggemann, *Genesis* (Louisville, KY: Westminster
 John Knox, 1982), p. 68.

17 Nelson, *Unashamed*, p. 161.

6 Jesus and shame

 1 Kenneth E. Bailey, *Jesus through Middle-Eastern Eyes: Cultural
 Studies in the Gospels* (Downers Grove, IL: IVP Academic,
 2008), p. 202.

 2 Bailey, *Jesus through Middle-Eastern Eyes*, p. 243.

 3 Angie O'Gorman, 'The Universe Bends Towards Justice', p. 242,
 cited in Walter Wink, *Engaging the Powers* (Minneapolis, MN:
 Fortress Press, 2017), p. 249.

 4 Donald Capps, *The Depleted Self: Sin in a Narcissistic Age*
 (Minneapolis, MN: Fortress Press, 1993), p. 164.

 5 Jerome H. Neyrey, *Honor and Shame in the Gospel of Matthew*
 (Louisville, KY: Westminster John Knox, 1998), pp. 165ff.

 6 Neyrey, *Honor and Shame in the Gospel of Matthew*, p. 181.
 See also Neyrey, 'Jesus, Gender and the Gospel of Matthew',
 Semeia 45 (2003), pp. 43–66.

 7 Brené Brown, *I Thought it Was Just Me (But it Isn't): Making
 the Journey from 'What Will People Think? to 'I Am Enough'*
 (New York, NY: Gotham, 2007), p. 280.

 8 Kosuke Koyama, *Three Mile an Hour God* (London: SCM Press,
 1979), p. 8.

 9 Neyrey, *Honor and Shame in the Gospel of Matthew*, p. 203.

10 Neyrey, *Honor and Shame in the Gospel of Matthew*, p. 212.

11 Neyrey, *Honor and Shame in the Gospel of Matthew*, p. 221.

12 C. Norman Kraus, *Jesus Christ Our Lord: Christology from a Disciple's Perspective* (Scottdale: Herald Press, 1990), p. 216.

13 Jerome Neyrey, 'Despising the Shame of the Cross: Honor and Shame in the Johannine Passion Narrative', *Semeia*, 68 (1994): 113–37.

14 Neyrey, 'Despising the shame of the cross'.

15 David A. DeSilva, *Honor, Patronage, Kinship & Purity: Unlocking New Testament Culture* (Downers Grove, IL: InterVarsity Press, 2000), p. 63.

7 'I could have died of embarrassment'

1 Michael Lewis, *Shame: The Exposed Self* (New York, NY: Free Press 1995), p. 75.

2 Lewis, *Shame: The Exposed Self*, p. 35.

3 Léon Wurmser, *The Mask of Shame* (Northvale, NJ: Jason Aronson Inc, 1994), p. 54.

4 Thomas Scheff, 'The Shame-Rage Spiral: A Case Study of an Interminable Quarrel', in Helen Block Lewis (ed.), *The Role of Shame in Symptom Formation* (Hillsdale, NJ: Erlbaum, 1987), pp. 109–50.

5 Lewis, *Shame: The Exposed Self*, p. 132.

6 Léon Wurmser, *The Mask of Shame*, p. 84.

7 Afif Sarhan and Caroline Davies, 'My daughter deserved to die for falling in love', *The Guardian*, 11 May 2008, available at <https://www.theguardian.com/world/2008/may/11/iraq. humanrights>.

8 Jane Hailé, *Honour Killing, Its Causes & Consequences: Suggested Strategies for the European Parliament*, Policy Department External Policies Briefing Paper, European Parliament, Brussels, 20 December 2007, available at <http:// www.europarl.europa.eu/meetdocs/2004_2009/documents/

dv/droi_2627052008_honourkilling/droi_2627052008_
honourkillingen.pdf>.

9 Particularly Suzanne Retzinger, 1987, 'Resentment of Laughter:
Video Studies of the Shame-rage Spiral', in Helen Block Lewis
(ed.), *The Role of Shame in Symptom Formation* (Hillsdale, NJ:
Erlbaum, 1987), pp. 151–81.

10 Sarhan and Davies, 'My daughter deserved to die for falling
in love'.

11 David Lewis, *The Unseen Face of Japan* (Gloucester: Wide
Margin, 2013), p. 203.

12 Inazo Nitobe, *Bushido: The Soul of Japan. The Code of the
Samurai* (Tokyo: The Student Company, 1905), p. 105.

13 Ruth Benedict, *The Chrysanthemum and the Sword: Patterns
of Japanese Culture* (Boston, MA: Houghton Mifflin, 1989),
p. 166.

14 C. Norman Kraus, *Jesus Christ Our Lord: Christology from a
Disciple's Perspective* (Herald Press, Scottdale, 1990), p. 212.

15 Jerome H. Neyrey, *Honor and Shame in the Gospel of Matthew*
(Louisville, KY: Westminster John Knox, 1998), p. 117.

16 Maura Campbell, 'Symbol and Reality: Water, Life, Death and
Christian Baptism', *Dialogue & Alliance*, 4(1) (1990): 48–60.

17 Cyril of Jerusalem, 'On the Rites of Baptism', in *Mystagogical
Catechesis*, 2:2.

8 The new life

1 Bruce J. Malina and John J. Pilch, *Social-Science Commentary
on the Letters of Paul* (Minneapolis, MI: Augsburg Fortress,
2006), p. 82.

2 John J. Pilch and Bruce J. Malina (eds), *Handbook of Biblical
Social Values* (Eugene, OR: Wipf and Stock Publishers, 2016),
p. 43.

3 N. T. Wright, '1 Corinthians', in *New Testament for Everyone* (Louisville, KY: Westminster John Knox, 2011), p. 64.

4 C. Norman Kraus, *Jesus Christ Our Lord: Christology from a Disciple's Perspective* (Herald Press, Scottdale, 1990), p. 241.

5 Jayson Georges and Mark D. Baker, *Ministering in Honor-Shame Cultures* (Downers Grove, IL: IVP Academic, 2016), p. 178.

6 Dale Martin, *The Corinthian Body* (New Haven, CT: Yale University Press, 1999), p. 96.

7 Patricia Toland, 'How Venezuelan Church Leaders' Behaviors Manifest Cultural Values of Honor and Shame in Their Interactions with Church Members' (PhD Diss., Biola University, 2015), p. 165.

8 Toland, 'How Venezuelan Church Leaders' Behaviors Manifest Cultural Values of Honor and Shame', p. 296.

9 Joel Green and Mark Baker, *Recovering the Scandal of the Cross: Atonement in New Testament and Contemporary Contexts* (Carlisle: Paternoster, 2000), p. 160.

10 Michael Lewis, *Shame: The Exposed Self* (New York, NY: Free Press, 1995), pp. 131–7.

11 Lewis, *Shame: The Exposed Self*, pp. 131–3.

12 John A. Forrester, *Grace for Shame: The Forgotten Gospel* (Toronto: Pastor's Attic Press, 2010), pp. 198–9.

13 Lewis, *Shame: The Exposed Self*, p. 135.

14 Forrester, *Grace for Shame*, pp. 220–48.

9 Me, you and shame

1 Brené Brown, *I Thought It Was Just Me (but It Isn't): Making the Journey from 'What Will People Think?' to 'I Am Enough'* (New York, NY: Gotham, 2007), p. 3.

2 Simon P. Walker, *Leading Out of Who You Are* (Carlisle: Piquant Editions, 2007), pp. 25–6.

3 Perry Shaw, 'Vulnerable Authority: A Theological Approach to Leadership and Teamwork', *Christian Education Journal*, 3(1) (2006): 119–33.

4 Shaw, 'Vulnerable Authority'.

5 Robert Jewett (ed.), *The Shame Factor* (Eugene, OR: Cascade, 2011), p. 3.

6 Philip Larkin (1922–85), 'This Be the Verse', 1971, in *High Windows*. Copyright © Estate of Philip Larkin. Used with permission of Faber and Faber Ltd.

7 Michael Lewis, *Shame: The Exposed Self* (New York, NY: Free Press, 1995), p. 113.

8 Lewis, *Shame: The Exposed Self*, pp. 111–12.

9 Alice Miller, *The Drama of the Gifted Child* (New York, NY: Basic Books, 1981), pp. 67ff.

10 Perry Shaw, *Transforming Theological Education* (Carlisle: Langham Global Library, 2014), p. 263.

11 Shaw, *Transforming Theological Education*, p. 210.

10 Ministering to the shamed

1 Bruce Waltke, *Genesis: A Commentary* (Grand Rapids, MI: Zondervan, 2001), p. 97.

2 The word 'sin' does appear in the story of Cain, where God tells Cain that 'sin is crouching at your door' (4:7). But it's a very strange verse. The Hebrew sentence is 'out of shape . . . incomprehensible' and 'very corrupt' (Westermann, *Genesis 1–11*, p. 299); the word 'sin' does not agree grammatically with the participle 'crouching', and so some commentators believe that the word was added later. (See Carly L. Crouch, 'תאטה as Interpolative Gloss: A Solution to Gen 4,7', *Zeitschrift für die*

alttestamentliche Wissenschaft, 123 (2011): 250–58.) If that's correct, then the first uncontested use of the word 'sin' is in Genesis 13:13.

3 John Forrester, *Grace for Shame: The Forgotten Gospel* (Toronto: Pastor's Attic Press, 2010), p. 221.

4 No pun intended.

5 Forrester, *Grace for Shame*, p. 221.

6 Dietrich Bonhoffer, (trans. John W. Doberstein), *Life Together* (London: SCM Press, 2015 edition), p. 72.

7 Heather Davis Nelson. *Unashamed: Healing Our Brokenness and Finding Freedom from Shame* (Wheaton, IL: Crossway, 2016), p. 155.

8 Morgan Lee, 'My Larry Nassar Testimony Went Viral. But There's More to the Gospel Than Forgiveness', *Christianity Today*, 31 January 2018, available at <https://www. christianitytoday.com/ct/2018/january-web-only/rachael-denhollander-larry-nassar-forgiveness-gospel.html>.